Voices at the World's Edge

First published in 2010 by
The Dedalus Press
13 Moyclare Road
Baldoyle
Dublin 13
Ireland

www.dedaluspress.com

Managing Editor: Pat Boran

This selection copyright © Dedalus Press, 2010
Foreword copyright © Marie Heaney, 2010
Editor's Introduction copyright © Paddy Bushe, 2010
All poems and essays copyright © the various contributors, 2010
Photographs, including cover image, copyright © John Minihan
Acknowledgements on p. 4 constitute an extension of this notice.

ISBN 978 1 906614 35 5 (paperback)
ISBN 978 1 906614 36 2 (hardbound)

All rights reserved.
No part of this publication may be reproduced in any form or by any means
without the prior written permission of the publisher.

Dedalus Press titles are distributed in the UK by
Central Books, 99 Wallis Road, London E9 5LN
and in North America by Syracuse University Press, Inc.,
621 Skytop Road, Suite 110, Syracuse, New York 13244.

Printed in Ireland by ColourBooks Ltd.

The Dedalus Press receives financial assistance from
The Arts Council / An Chomhairle Ealaíon

Voices at the World's Edge
Irish Poets on Skellig Michael

❦

EDITOR
Paddy Bushe

FOREWORD
Marie Heaney

PHOTOGRAPHS
John Minihan

DEDALUS PRESS
DUBLIN, IRELAND

ACKNOWLEDGEMENTS

Acknowledgements and thanks are due to the editors of the following in which a number of the poems included herein first appeared:

An Guth, Irish Pages, Poetry Ireland Review and *Southword.*

'Skellig Michael' and 'Strange Company' from *Only This Room* (2009) by Kerry Hardie by kind permission of the author and The Gallery Press www.gallerypress.com

'Vertigo' and 'The Litany' from *The Sun-fish* by Eiléan Ní Chuilleanáin by kind permisssion of the author and The Gallery Press www.gallerypress.com

'Sceilig Bay' and 'At the Butler Arms' by Derek Mahon from *An Autumn Wind* by kind permission of the author and The Gallery Press www.gallerypress.com

Voices at the World's Edge
Irish Poets on Skellig Michael

Note from Grellan D. Rourke
Heritage Service, Office of Public Works

Skellig Michael is a unique place. It is a place of profound spirit and a remarkable survival of an early medieval monastic settlement. The monuments on the island are the tangible remains of outstanding human achievement representing many centuries of continuous construction and habitation. Their physical presence is intense; there is a special communion with the striking topography of the island. It is a place set apart from modern-day life, a place for contemplation.

We are honoured to be guardians of this place and work to preserve it for future generations so they will continue to marvel at its magnificence. Conservation and preservation works to the access steps, the monastery and the hermitage are coming to a close after three decades. During that time Skellig has given up much information about its past. When on this island no month goes by without new information coming to light. Little by little layers of the past have been uncovered and our knowledge has been enriched considerably in the process of excavation, preservation and study.

It seems fitting to mark the close of these works in an appropriate way. By something, which not just captures the spirit of the place but something, which is inspired by the place itself. Poetry provides the best medium. Skellig Michael is not just a historic entity but can inspire the future as it does here. Because it is such a visually stunning place the inclusion of black and white photography also seems appropriate.

This is a project, which emanated from the island itself. It is a celebration of the power and spirit of this place and its ability to generate new influences, to reach beyond physical limitation.

September 2010

Contents

🕊

Foreword by Marie Heaney / 11
Editor's Introduction / 19
A fine soft morning on Sceilig Bay, trans. Derek Mahon / 23

🕊

PADDY BUSHE
Skellig Birds / 27
Entrance / 29
Climbing the Eye of the Needle, South Peak / 30
Illuminated Manuscript / 31
Eadarlúid Oíche Gaoithe / 32
Interval on a Windy Night / 33
Fardoras / 34
Lintel / 35
Oileánú / 38
Islanding / 39
Stormbound / 40
The Dragons and Archangels of Skellig Michael / 42

JOHN F. DEANE
Night on Skellig Michael / 45
Skellig / 49

THEO DORGAN
Sailing to the Edge / 55

KERRY HARDIE
A High Tradition / 65
Reading Heinrich Boll's *The Clown* on a bus
bound for Skellig Michael / 79
Skellig Michael / 80
Sky Station / 81
Strange Company / 82

BIDDY JENKINSON
Bun na Faille / 84
Smál / 84
Clochán / 84
Suí Fhionan / 85
Sólás / 85
An Manach agus an Chailleach Nite Éadaigh / 86
Brionglóid Sceilge / 87
Limistéir / 88
The Last Holy Woman of Sceilg / 89
An Cat Mara / 100

SEÁN LYSAGHT
Gannets / 105
Storm Petrels / 106

EILÉAN NÍ CHUILLEANÁIN
Vertigo / 111

NUALA NÍ DHOMHNAILL
Díseart na Sceilge / 120
Skellig Hermitage / 121
Éanlaith na Sceilge / 124
Birds of Skellig / 125
Annálacha Díseart na Sceilge / 130
The Annals of the Skellig Hermitage / 131

BERNARD O'DONOGHUE
Out in the Weather / 141
Weather / 148
The Skellig Listeners / 151

CATHAL Ó SEARCAIGH
Sa Mhainistir / 154
In the Monastery / 155
Ceathrúintí Thuathal Mac Liag / 156
Tuathal Mac Liag's Quatrains / 157
Tuathal ag Cuimhneamh ar Chaomhán / 162
Tuathal Daydreams Caomhán / 163
Tuathal ag Mealladh Chaomháin / 164
Tuathal Seduces Caomhán / 165
Paidir Thuathail / 166
Tuathal's Prayer / 167

MACDARA WOODS
Timesis / 171
In the Light of Whipple's Moon / 183

At the Butler Arms, by Derek Mahon / 185

Notes on Contributors / 187

Foreword

Marie Heaney

❦

The Skelligs rise out of the sea, remote and mysterious. From the distance they seem as uninhabitable as icebergs. But the larger of the two islands, Skellig Michael, was inhabited for over 600 years by hermits, anchorites, holy men who wanted the solitude and altitude of the place to bring them nearer to their God. And today, weather permitting, visitors flock to spend an afternoon in this elemental place.

The history, mythology and geographical wonders of Skellig Michael make it a natural magnet for writers, and for this anthology eleven poets and a photographer visited the island and had the privilege, as I had, of spending a night or more there. They write about that experience in ways that are as unique, enigmatic and multi-faceted as the island itself.

Out of their pilgrimage come nature poems, love poems, religious poems, a translation from the Irish as well as many original poems in Irish itself. There are prose pieces that are descriptive, reflective and philosophical and one by Biddy Jenkinson that is humorous—a clever pastiche of early monastic writing—and ironically relevant to our times.

A sequence of poems by Cathal Ó Searcaigh has its origin in a dream that he had while on the island and is written in the voice of monk living in the monastery in the earliest times, a disaffected, unbelieving young man who is separated from his lover and is revolted by the monastic life he is forced to lead.

Another thought-provoking piece concentrates on the communal nature of the monastic settlement rather than the sense of isolation that it often evokes. Macdara Woods sees it as a shared space—"A space for living long-term, for living with, and in spite of, the foibles of others"—and as he enters the monastery he is struck by "the sheer urban cohesion of it, in the same way as when you enter into one of those walled Italian hill-towns that from below look as tight and impregnable as an oyster".

Kerry Hardie has a meditative piece on the effect and purpose, the pros and cons of the isolation and asceticism sought by the monks who built the monastery—"minds hungry for God" in the words of Theo Dorgan—and its relevance to modern meditative living.

Being in this otherworldly place inevitably brings most of the poets to reflect on the fundamentals of human existence: time and eternity, the past and the future, faith and unbelief. Some are ambushed by memories that transport them to distant times and places. Others have experiences that border on the visionary. Every one of them testifies to the intensity of their experience on the island. All of them seemed to have been changed in some way by being there.

I will never forget my own visit there or that marvellous moment when I caught my first glimpse of the islands rising from the water, remote and austere. Unthinkable that anyone could live there; incredible that anyone would *choose* to live there. "The most fantastic and impossible rock in the world," as George Bernard Shaw described it.

I was brought out in Eoin Walsh's boat, one of the last two wooden ones that make the long and rolling journey from Portmagee. The crossing was relatively calm, unlike that of Tomás Rua O'Súilleabháin, whose nineteenth century poem about the attempted journey in a storm is translated by Derek Mahon, who has also written his own poem about not getting to the island. Calm or not, I was still very glad to arrive on Skellig Michael and to be on *terra firma* again. When I set foot there it felt, if anything, more mysterious than it had seemed from the land and I had a sense of the numinous—as if I had landed on Prospero's island.

"An island fortress on the world's edge" is how Theo Dorgan describes Skellig Michael, and to look up at cliffs that rise almost sheer for seven hundred feet, knowing that you must climb to the top, is a singular challenge. As I started my ascent to the monastic settlement on the North Peak, I could only marvel at the asceticism, the faith, the wish to be nearer their God that had driven men to live in this place over a period of 600 years. Still, in spite of the starkness of the terrain and the fundamentalism that it mirrored, I felt a certain benignity in the atmosphere.

Beautiful and amazing as the monastery on the summit is, perhaps the greatest wonder on the island is the six hundred or so steps that bring you there. Paddy Bushe has previously described them as

> A great snake scaling
> Towards the heights, insinuating
> Itself into the island.

Climbing those steps was physically easier than I expected. I took lots of contemplative pauses on the way to admire the distant views and to reflect with a kind of incredulity on the tenacity and endurance of the generations of monks who had cut these steps from the rocks. And on the devotion of the thousands of pilgrims over the centuries who had made this same ascent.

I was stopped in my tracks, too, by the striking rock formations that marked the way up. Most striking of all, perhaps, the one so aptly called 'the wailing woman'. Bernard O'Donoghue writes: "The impression of this worn cross—disturbing at the best of times—has gained a new grimness by its resemblance now to the tortured, electrode-wearing figure from Abu Ghraib." Past and present shuttling through each other—a constant motif throughout this anthology.

The sense of achievement I felt as I approached the summit was completely eclipsed by amazement at the unexpectedly sudden appearance of the settlement. The symmetry and in-placeness of the beehive huts, the oratories, the crosses, the grave yard and the breathtaking views beyond them made me realise I had arrived at a unique destination: "the rounded skulls of eremite cells / creased by winter storms, spring tempests" that, in John F. Deane's words, had once housed "those who lost their lives to win them back". I was in awe, too, of the survival skills of these men. With no spring wells for water they had to devise other means. The runnels they cut into the rocks to collect water have been mentioned in a number of poems and have become a metaphor in Eiléan Ní Chuilleanáin's poem 'Vertigo':

> The soaking tears of centuries drill down
> Low passages in between the stones....

Foreword ❦ 13

As I walked around this extraordinary space my wonder was matched by the serenity I felt: man and nature in harmony everywhere I looked—and inside one of the huts a living manifestation of this. As my eyes got used to the darkness, I saw a Manx Shearwater sitting on her eggs. Birds, of course, are one of the many wonders of the Skelligs and had been there for millennia when the first hermits landed, but modern technology has discovered something that even the most observant monk would have found hard to verify: this bird has been ringed so we know for sure that she has returned to this sanctuary to hatch her eggs for a number of years.

On my way up I felt as if I was being attended by puffins; they are so numerous on Skellig Michael that they have become its unofficial emblem. They were much smaller than I expected and comical "with the faces of Marcel Marceau" as Macdara Woods puts it. They looked out at me from under stones or surveyed me calmly from the walls and made me smile with their ratchety call and their ungainly takeoffs and landings and their bustly flight, a complete contrast to the jet-propelled dive-bombing of the gannets, or the indolent glide of the gulls. But I found out that the comic-postcard appearance of these little creatures was deceptive: their lives are as elemental as the island they return to after wintering out for six months at sea.

Like the islands themselves this anthology is alive with birds. Poet after poet writes about them: Paddy Bushe and Nuala Ní Dhomhnaill both have poems devoted entirely to the birds of Skellig. Seán Lysaght gives us portraits of two of them: the storm petrels who live in the walls of the monastery and whose gurgle is one of the most distinctive sounds on the island, and the gannets visiting the island from their fortress on the Little Skellig:

> Rich neighbours
> Sailing their big yachts
> All over the sound.

On our way back to Portmagee we sailed close to Little Skellig—another experience of a lifetime. Twenty thousand pairs of gannets live there: the rock gleams white with guano and they perch on every ledge of the rockface, looking down on us as imperturbably as those marble choirs of seraphim and cherubim carved on the façades of medieval cathedrals.

The monks were not the only ones to cut pathways into the rocks of Skellig Michael. In the early nineteenth century, two lighthouses were built on the western side of the island, one high up and soon afterwards a second one lower down. The lighthouse men made pathways to the lighthouses, broader and safer than those the monks had made, but they had used dynamite and the holes are still visible in the rock face alongside the path. The higher lighthouse—the Old Lighthouse—has fallen into ruin but it is still an impressive structure. The equally impressive New Lightouse now sends out an automatic signal and it is closed off to visitors, but I was privileged again because Richard Foran, a lighthouse keeper, was there doing maintenance work and with great grace and hospitality, he brought us on a tour of the lighthouse. It was a wonderfully warm and reassuring space and it was fascinating to see the enormous glass slats at the top of the lighthouse that magnified the rays of a small light bulb and sent them miles across the bay.

I felt a real sense of achievement when I reached the monastic settlement on the eastern summit but, as it turns out, that is the easy option. The more demanding and dangerous pilgrimage is to the South Peak. We had got close to this area as we climbed to the Old Lighthouse, a precipitous enough climb in itself, and from there could see above us the remains of a recently re-discovered hermitage, even more remote and inaccessible.

The very names of the rock formations, the Spit, the Needle's Eye, give some idea of the challenging and perilous climb the poets and pilgrims faced. An account by one Charles Smith written in 1756 describes the pilgrimage. At the second stage the pilgrims arrive at a formation "by some called the spindle, by others the spit; which is a long, narrow fragment of the rock, projecting from the summit of this frightful place, over a raging sea; and this is walked to, by a narrow path of only two feet in breadth, and several steps in length. Here the devotees, women as well as men, get astride on this rock, and so edge forward until they arrive at a stone cross, which some bold adventurer cut formerly on its extreme end: and here, having repeated a pater noster, returning from thence concludes the penance."

It is presumed that one or more hermits, even more zealous than their brethren, broke away from the main settlement, cut out the steps to this eyrie and built a hermitage there even closer to God. Tradition has it moreover that the monks from the main monastery took refuge here from the Viking raids.

I did not make it to the South Peak, and having read Charles Smith's account cannot say I regret it. Many of the poets included here did face that perilous climb, a pilgrimage that invariably proved memorable and significant.

In 'The Annals of The Skellig Hermitage', Nuala Ní Dhomhnaill describes her ascent:

> With ropes attached, and calmed by the support of
> the initiates, this poor pilgrim climbed the South
> Peak. It was a pet day, and light gleamed on the ocean,
> a silver shield reflecting the sunlight. Horror and fear
> fell away from me, panic and terror left me. Although
> each step I climbed was like a step to my own death,
> I came down like a cat. I could cling to the rock like
> a limpet. I understood the hermits, their celebratory
> universe. Their pride, too, I understood.

While we were visiting the lighthouses, we witnessed, from that unique vantage point, something that might, in jest, be called a Viking raid in reverse. It did, however, bring to mind the dread those monks, on that same vantage point centuries ago, must have experienced as they saw the long, dragon-headed ships enter stealthily into the sound.

It so happened that the Volvo round-the-world yacht race was taking place and a yacht called the Green Dragon, with a joint crew of Irish and Chinese yachtsmen aboard, was taking part. The boats had been in Galway for a few festive days and the next leg of the race was taking them to Stockholm. It was evening and the visitors had gone. There was a good stiff breeze blowing and I was glad that I was staying on the island. Suddenly we saw a yacht scudding along. As it came closer we saw on the full sail a heraldic green dragon.

We were delighted. We became even more excited when we saw that it was in the lead and realised that one of the crew, a local man from Derrynane who had sailed these waters since childhood, had taken a different route from most of the other yachts. By the time they hove into view, sailing between the two Skelligs, the Green Dragon was a small speck on the horizon, heading for Scandinavia. Paddy Bushe writes about it in his poem 'The Dragons and Archangels of Skellig Michael':

> And so it was that Seal Cove all at once
> Held its breath when that emblazoned sail,
> Familiar from that otherworld of television,
> Flared out of the west, waking the sunset.

Skellig Michael is one of the most extraordinary and beautiful places in the world. In Keats' words it "dost tease us out of thought as doth eternity". It is challenging to write about it, impossible to comprehend fully all that it stands for. Poet after poet attests to this. They write about intense and radiant moments, experiences that have carried them beyond the borders of the usual.

Kerry Hardie's poem 'Strange Company' describes the South Peak hermitage and what she felt there.

> There was a platform, a sea-eagle's rake.
> A seam chipped in bare rock to channel rain.
> A ledge that straddled space, creating place.
> Blue sheepsbit scabious in the sandy grit.
>
> Someone used my eyes to look.
> Someone used my heart to soar.
> No one spoke to me of death.
> Death belongs to time and time was not.

Introduction

Above all, I remember climbing the South Peak—three of us, terrified, astounded, elated poets—guided with infinite patience by Grellan and Alan to a place I had been convinced for twenty years that I would never get to. It was a bright, boisterous day in June 2008, and, on a precarious hermitage hung high over the sea moving below us, we sat and, above all, we marvelled. The three of us have written about that particular climb for this book. It was the first day of what turned out to be a series of extraordinary and multi-faceted visits by a group of Irish poets and a photographer, the creative results of which you are holding in your hands. Not all of the poets got to the South Peak. Not all of us got to the lighthouses. Not all of us got to see puffins, or storm petrels. But our collective experience was always edging towards the miraculous, physical and spiritual, and we have borne poetic witness to this.

Grellan Rourke, Senior Conservation Architect with the OPW and the guiding official spirit on the island, is the "onlie begetter" of this book. When he approached me some three years ago to discuss a project to mark the end of the OPW work on the Early Medieval remains, I grasped the opportunity to try something which had long been at the back of my mind. Skellig Michael has been a presence on the Irish literary horizon for many years, sometimes even for writers who had never been there. A group of a dozen or so Irish poets, staying in twos and threes for a few days on the island, would surely be creatively invigorated and come up with something worthy of this most extraordinary and mysterious place. Grellan was enthusiastic and the project was launched, with legendary literary photographer John Minihan added to the mix.

Just one photographer, but getting the right mix of poets to the island was more complex. I was anxious that varying poetic perspectives be brought to Skellig—linguistic, philosophical, gender, subject matter, style … in short, that the resulting work should be representative of the best of contemporary Irish poetry. The whole thing was further complicated by the fact that the visits took place in the summers of 2008 and, enforcedly, 2009, two of the wettest and windiest summers I can remember. There were many consequent postponements and cancellations. This not only prolonged the whole process but meant that some poets who envisaged taking part could not do so in the end. Some poets would like to have gone, but understandable fears of the sea or of heights eventually dissuaded them. The logistics of the project, in other words, did not enjoy divine intervention, at least none with benign intent. This was perhaps salutary. In my own case, I was stormbound on the island for five days, a wonderful and productive stay which led to a number of the poems in this book. There were other fine poets whom I would have liked to include, but could not accommodate. In particular, I regret that I could not include my personal and professional poet-friends in Kerry. They, however, are in a better position than most to visit Sceilg Mhichíl when they wish.

I don't intend to make any comments about the individual contributions, which Marie Heaney has already touched on with a sensitivity heightened by her own stay on the island. There are just a few clarifications I need to make. The translations of Nuala Ní Dhomhnaill and Cathal Ó Searcaigh are my own, with the poets' approval. They are as close to the originals as I could be; I am not a believer in "free" translation. Biddy Jenkinson prefers not to have her poetry translated, and I respect that position. Derek Mahon had hoped to get to Skellig, but time and the weather intervened. However, as a result of his visit to Iveragh, he did a wonderful translation of 'Maidin Bhog Álainn' by the Iveragh poet Tomás Rua Ó Súilleabháin, a poem (and a great song) about the narrow escape of a group of pilgrims almost drowned as they made for "carraig glas ard na naomh" or Sceilg Mhichíl. Subsequently I heard Derek read his own poem about *not* getting to Skellig, and he has been good enough to allow these two pieces to bookend this anthology. I hope these pieces are merely preliminary to a successful visit.

There are many people, apart from the writers and the photographer, to whom thanks is due for helping to bring this book into the world. Foremost among these are the OPW staff who take care of Skellig Michael with extraordinary integrity, dedication and insight. I have already mentioned Grellan Rourke, who instigated the project and who guided it skillfully through the corridors of power, together with Dermot Burke in the OPW head office. We faint-hearted poets have good reason to thank both Grellan and archaeologist Alan Hayden for their time and patience with us, especially when scaling the South Peak. Their range and depth of knowledge enormously enhanced our experience, and their commitment is inspirational. I personally saw them working a twelve-hour day on the South Peak during continuous wind and rain. The OPW guides, Bob Harris, Head Guide, Eamonn Lowe, Catherine Merrigan, Claire O'Halloran and Maggie Prendiville, who choose year after year to come back during the season, bear courteous and informative witness to the cumulative enchantment of Skellig Michael. The sensitive and authentic conservation work which the OPW has carried out would not be possible without the skill and dedication of OPW workers Patrick O'Shea, foreman, Tom Kerrisk, John Lyne, Michael O'Connor and Colin McGorlick, safety advisor. We must also thank them for the use of their huts while they were ashore at weekends. Eoin Walsh, whose boat is the OPW carrier, was always courteous and helpful, even when nail-biting Munster Finals on a crackly radio threatened the evenness of his keel! Also, embodying another fascinating aspect of the continuing story of Skellig Michael, lighthouse guardians Richard Foran and Raymond Wickham were beacons of information for the poets who were lucky enough to have their visit coincide with the now, alas, occasional presence of these men.

Of course there is no book without a publisher. Pat Boran of Dedalus Press was unable to make it to Skellig Michael as a poet. But he embraced the project as publisher with his usual enthusiasm and expertise, and has contributed continually and enormously to the whole project.

This is not in any sense a book "about" Skellig Michael. It does not set out to give any comprehensive picture of the island, its wildlife or its historical background. It is the creative reaction of a dozen or so artists to their visit there. There are many published works—novels, poems, guidebooks, documentary radio and television material, scholarly books, historical and annalistic references etc.—which can be used by those who wish to research the island further. Indeed I would hope this book might encourage such research, as well as presenting its own, necessarily fragmentary and personal insights into Skellig Michael.

Is pribhléid thar an ngáthach é turas a thabhairt ar Sceilg Mhichíl. Is pribhléid níos neamhghnáthaí fós bheith in ann fanacht ann thar oíche. Agus is pribhléid ghairmiúil do aon scríbhneoir an deis sin a thapú chun cur lena chuid oibre. Tá súil agam go bhfuil luach na pribhléide sin le sonrú ar a bhfuil sa leabhar seo.

Together with the other writers and the photographer, I have shared in the personal and professional privilege it has been to take part in this project. For most people, just to get to Skellig is unforgettable. We have had the privilege of an extended stay—several of them, in my own case. I hope the reader will find some sense of that extraordinary privilege in these pages.

Paddy Bushe
Bá na Scealg, 01/07/2010

A fine soft morning on Sceilig Bay

*One fine, soft morning—St. Michael's Day—
Communion-bound in the Sceilig Bay,
we watched as the breakers multiplied,
rain threatened and a strong wind blew.
We wisely decided on turning back
and finding harbour beyond Bray Head;
starting up when I heard the crew,
I who'd been dozing was wide awake.*

*Our seine-boat was a delight that morning,
high in the waves, six oars at work,
the sail full and the rowlocks slick,
every board was alive and singing.
We'd held her fast in the flying foam
surging and sparkling beneath the beam;
no stir on the water from here to Dingle
until we made for St. Michael's Rock—*

*when Sow Cliff there on the port side
shrieked fit to be tied, Gull Sound
roared aloud like a bull in pain,
the Groaner groaned in the howling wind.
Thanks be to Jesus we weren't drowned
and stretched in the dark depths of the tide
but spared for another, quieter run
when, please God, we might try again.*

*The priest prayed wildly in the stern
to spare the boat and save the men,
and he must have been heard in heaven above
as the white wave-crests crashed over us
for we cleared Rincarragh in due course
with the Narrows a flat calm after the sea;
so we kept on till we came to shore
and broached a barrel at Seán Magee's.*

*God, we were shook, so we sat all night
and emptied the porter, watching the gale
from that warm room until first light
and giving thanks for our lucky escape.
Ribbed, tarred and finished by Seán O'Neilll,
that little boat will never know harm:
where would you find a finer ship
to deliver you safe from such a storm.*

Translated by Derek Mahon
from the Irish of Tomás Rua Ó Súilleabháin
1785–1848

Paddy Bushe

Skellig Birds

PUFFIN
Hilarious, yes,
But that sad clown spends winters
Completely at sea.

FULMAR
Looks like the others
But it spits independence
And will not be gulled.

SHEARWATER
Those aerobatics,
Skimming the froth off the waves,
Live up to its name.

PEREGRINE
When its tapered wings
Stir to plunge from the high ledge
Fledgling hearts plummet.

ROCK PIPITS
They're grey against stone
But they cheep and wag their tails,
Mad for attention.

CHOUGHS
Shrieking a cancan
They display their scarlet legs
To the whole wide world.

Pigeons
Sometimes they arrive,
Lost souls looking for a new
Sense of direction.

Herring Gull
Such a common name!
The red spot on its beak glows
With indignation.

Kittiwakes
At Blind Man's Cove
They scream their names loud enough
To waken the dead.

Guillemot
Ridiculous name,
But it's what the guide-book says,
There, in black and white.

Cormorants
Totally immersed,
They yearn for a christening
Other than *sea-hag*.

Storm Petrels
Holed up in stone walls
Warmly safe from the world's storms,
You hear them gurgle.

Gannets
Wheeling in sunlight,
On those glorious white wings—
What is left to say?

Entrance

for John F. Deane

Was this, a poet asked from afar,
God's city, the pleroma? And yes, yes,
That otherwordly plenitude lives here,
Infusing pavements and oratories and cells
With the numinosum they aspired to.
Here stone expands with more than it encloses,
Embodies horizons that widen like ripples.

But here too is this world's proclamation:
Marvel at these bouldered walls as you bend
Beneath the huge lintel of the entrance.
Know your own fragility as you climb each
Step towards entry into this citadel.
Know that herein only lies your safety,
Subjecting your self to the Self of God.

And here is Holy Rule and Inquisition
Inherent beneath the weight of stone.
Here is plenitude codified, here are chains
And edicts: here, also, is the triumph of fear.

Climbing the Eye of the Needle, South Peak

for Alan Hayden

The Needle's Eye, already well threaded
With safety-ropes, opened like a sleeve
Above us. Could I pull myself through,
Draw the world inside out and discover
The light beyond, like that long ago child
Daring the darkness of his huge pullover?
The sea, dizzily beneath us, heaved disbelief.

Here was the *hand over hand over foothold*
To God I'd written achingly about. Now I recall
Only the coming up and out, the sunlit terrace
Trembling all over in the windy brightness,
And my whole self slipping easily through,
Some old saint's arm giving its reliquary
The slip, punching the air with delight.

Illuminated Manuscript

Last night I boiled the young sorrel leaves
I had gathered behind the monastery
In the afternoon, while the wind was rising.
And after supper I wrote for hours, my pen
And notebook pooled in the gas-lamp's light.
The gale battered my hut all night
While I worked and while, afterwards,
I slept, happy with what I had written.

And, although there was also tinned food,
Instant coffee, a solar-powered fridge
And mobile phone reception near the helipad,
For *supper*, read *collatio*,
For *hut:* read *cell* or *scriptorium*,
For *pen*, read *quill*,
For *notebook*, read *vellum*,
For *gas-lamp*, read *rush-light*,
For *pooled*, read *illuminated*.
And for *happy with what I had written*,
Read, with all due resistance,
Ad majorem Dei gloriam.

Eadarlúid Oíche Gaoithe

Ar sos siúlóide ón bpeannaireacht
Beirim ar thigh solais na Sceilge
Idir scamaill agus réaltanna
Ag uainíocht gaetha fada fuarchúiseacha
Ar thigh solais Oileán Doinn ó dheas.

Samhlaím Ir agus Donn ina mbun,
Cuimhní goirte sáile ag crá na beirte,
Iad ag breacadh cóid rúnda solais
Idir a chéile oileánach, dréachtanna seifte
Don athscríobh, don Leabhar Nua Gabhála.

Interval on a Windy Night

Strolling, on a break from writing,
I catch the Skellig lighthouse
Between clouds and stars
Alternating long, calculating beams
With the lighthouse on the Bull to the south.

I sense Ir and Donn behind all this,
Both tormented by bitter, salty memories,
Swapping secret coded messages
Between their islanded selves, draft plans
For the rewrite, for the New Book of Invasions.

Fardoras

do Grellan Rourke

Ar ardán scoite tamall amach leis féin
Atá an t-aireagal, mar a bheadh manach
A thuig gan postúlacht a thábhacht féin
I leith Dé agus i leith na mainistreach.
Cromtha isteach ar féin, caitheann sé uaidh
An ceobhrán atá á shileadh ag an oileán.

Gealann sé diaidh ar ndiaidh istigh
Sa domoladh tais, an braon beag anuas
Chomh rialta céanna le cloigín éatrom
I gciúnas an chaonaigh. Sníonn an solas
Idir an doras íseal agus an fhuinneog
A osclaíonn amach ar aer is ar fharraige.

Tá an fardoras leathan, leithead an earagail
Ó thaobh taobh sula gcúngaíonn sé,
Dingnithe isteach sna fallaí, ag iompar
Ualach cloch atá saoirsithe chun míne,
Chun bheith istigh leo féin, gan stró,
Mar éin in ealta, nó mar éisc i mbáire.

Sa leathdhorchadas, barra mo mhéaranna
Agus tóirse om threorú, rianaím amach
An chros faoi cheilt ar íochtar an fhardorais
Gurbh leac uaighe í tráth, leac an anamcharad
Ar shantaigh na manaigh é mar chloch taca
Coimhdeachta, chun díon a n-urnaithe

Lintel

for Grellan Rourke

On a terrace set a little while apart
You find the oratory, like a monk who knew
Without officiousness his own standing
In the eyes of God and of the monastery.
Hunched in on itself, it shoulders off
The mist that the island is shedding.

Little by little it brightens inside
In the damp and must, the drop down
As regularly timed as a tinkling bell
In the mossy silence. The light flows
Between the low doorway and the window
That opens out onto the sea and the air.

The lintel is broad, the breadth of the oratory
From side to side before it narrows,
Wedging itself into the walls, bearing
A weight of stones masoned into smoothness,
Into being at ease with themselves
Like birds in a flock, or fish in a shoal.

In the half-light, the tips of my fingers
And my torch as guides, I trace out
The cross hidden on the lintel's underside
That was once the gravestone of the anamchara
Whom the monks craved as a buttressing
Guardian, to lift the roof of their prayer

A thógáil suas ó fuaimint go firmimint,
Chun gath naofa solais a theilgean
Ar aon nathair a bheadh ag lúbarnaíl
Isteach nó amach faoi tháirseach a n-aigne,
Agus guailne leathana a mbráthar naofa
Ag iompar ualach a mbeatha os a gcionn.

From foundation up to firmament,
To lance a ray of sacred light
Towards any snake that would insinuate
Itself under or over their mind's threshold,
While the broad shoulders of their holy brother
Bore the weight of their lives overhead.

Oileánú

Tá an Sceilg iata ag an aimsir.
Gaoth ag éirí arís. Grian agus scamaill
In iomarbhá airgid agus luaidhe
Go geal éatrom, go dubh trom, fuadar
Agus fuirse faoin bhfarraige atá meáite
Ar oilean i ndiaidh oileain aonair
A chruthú ar dhromchla na cruinne.

Níl ann do Uíbh Ráthach ná Béara.
Ar fhíor na spéire, chím, ar éigin,
An Scairbh, Duibhinis, Oileán Dá Cheann
Ag síneadh uaim, smeadar i ndiaidh smeadair,
Ó dheas isteach sa gceo, amach san aimsir.
Mar sheilimide éigin farraige, cúngaím isteach
Ionam féin, im pheann luaidhe, insan oileán.

Islanding

Skellig is enclosed by the weather.
Wind rising again. Sunlight and clouds
In a silver and lead contest
Of airy light and heavy dark, a hustle
And bustle driving a sea that's determined
To create island after solitary island
All over the surface of the world.

Iveragh and Beara have disappeared.
On the horizon, I make out, just,
Scariff, Deenish, Two-headed Island,
Stretching from me, smudge after smudge,
Southward into the fog, out into the weather.
Like some sea-snail or other, I shrink
Into myself, into my pencil, into the island.

Stormbound

The fourth day running now
Without any sign of a boat,
And, ignoring the slap and thump
Of the wind, I stroll to the landing,
Wondering idly about a boat
Tomorrow. A young fulmar
Flaps, and spits straight at me
Its terror of being abandoned.
Then around the last sheltered
Bend above the pier I gape
At a sea that's gone out of its mind.

This is no swell, or tide,
Or crest, or trough or backwash
Ordained by moon and wind.
This is a charge, a hurtling,
A trampling, a goring, a huge
Grey and green and white bulk
Buckling, a frenzy to withdraw,
Heave breath, rear, re-gather
Itself, again, for the great collapse
Again, of itself and of cliffs
And of pier and of everything
Under the sun and moon and stars.

And all at once this raw, tormented air,
This roadway pounded by the knowledge
Of its own pitiful, tenuous hold,
This onlooker, aghast once again
At what he has always known,

Are all urgent with the need
For the stone steps' passage
To the high oratories and cells,
For ordained hours, for bells and ritual
That might placate the implacable,
For the final, clear word upon this rock.

The Dragons and Archangels of Skellig Michael

for Marie Heaney

We knew the race was coming from Galway
And had seen the sails high out to windward,
But a sharp northwesterly had edged us away
To the sheltered road between the lighthouses.

And so it was that Seal Cove all at once
Held its breath when that emblazoned sail,
Familiar from the otherworld of television,
Flared out of the west, waking the sunset.

Here was a presence wonderful beyond belief:
Here was communion, a congregation,
As if the Archangel Michael had abandoned
His solitary, high-peaked wrestling with monsters

For the time being, to descend and watch
That slanted, billowing exuberance burst
Into and out of our vision, to hear your daughter
In your excited phone speak from afar

And invoke the blessing of the Green Dragon
On all of us, on the guides high as kites,
On the beaming lighthouse-men, on the twilight
Replete with a grace proper to archangels.

John F. Deane

Night on Skellig Michael

St John's Eve on Bald Mountain

The small half-decker smelled of fish-blood and old oils; the engine
sputtered, died, then caught, a cough
of black smoke lifted towards the quay. Grey day, though calm
in the lee of land, but the waves and wash demanding

out on the open sea. Lift
and fall, sidelong
sluice, splashing of spray over the bow, loll and pitch
of the deck—

made me hold hard to the gunwale, its varnished and rounded wood
rough now as an aged hand. I was
temporal, temporary seafarer, legs braced, with an assumed
bravado.

It is a getting away, and a getting to. Extreme
islands, strict and overwhelming, dark-walled bastion. The skipper
scattered bread from his sandwich
to the white horses of the sea: you make offerings, he grinned,

to the god that keeps you. A gull
flipped its body over, swooped, and caught; I saw its yellow bill
with that small bloodberry, and its yellow eye
watchful. Atlantic patient then in the Blue Cove; Skellig

Michael, furious as that high archangel
who holds the entrance to the heart of God. Roots of the island
claw down into the fiery entrails of the earth, mother-
mountain, sacrament and threat. Awed

I began up the steep black steps
broken out of the ribs of rock, tripped, almost at once, my palm
scraping against loose shale, drops of blood
an early offering to the island. Looming above me

the torturous climb, up towards shadow. Difficult,
and tasking. I turned, often, to rest,
to watch out over the Atlantic, my breath filched
by the wind-touched silences, save

where the squabbling of kittiwakes on the cliff walls
spoke cacophonies of ego-bickering. I took
Mussorgsky into my hearing, that fire-ball shaman-music,
Night on Bald Mountain, to guide me

upwards with the energy of demons and the swift
flight of the furies. No delicate harmonies
here, no soft-pedalling, no mute. I sweated,
stomach heaved

with effort, am not as young …
I paused to see the tiny growths along rock walls, there
as if they have clung forever: sea-campion,
hawkbit, prickly cowthistle, pearlwort. I reached, wearied,

    ❧

the longed-for monastery remains at the rough-hewn edge
of heaven, at the sensuous ridge of Hell; the silent
abandoned praying-places, stone crosses

pitted by gales, the rounded skulls of eremite cells
creased by winter storms, spring tempests; lurking-nest
of the suffering soul, Mussorgsky, Ishmael, Ahab, Grimes …

    ❧

I stood a long time, shivering, summer, with the chill
of height and evening wind, with old disturbances

long settled in the dust under my feet. House of those
who lost their lives to win them back. The poem,

as the hermits did, raddles its being to find the soul:
source and sustenance, summit, spirit, end. I found

    ❧

shelter inside a cell, took from my rucksack
bread and whiskey, made of them my Eucharist, calling
on the Christ-name, my edible, drinkable God,

and knew my flesh and earth-flesh
suffused with the blood of Jesus. I lay down
on hard clay, and tried to sleep. Turned,

hurting, earth cold beneath me,
storm-petrel, shearwater
whispering their way into burrow and crevasse underground.

I turned at last into old darkness, Jesus
in the bloodstream, dreamed communion
of old saints, of anchorite, eremite, and was in tune.

※

Woke again, head hurting and body sore.
Horizons were touched with light

and all about the sea-birds soared and cried; I breakfasted,
bread, and a redeeming draught of whiskey. Down

at the landing-place I sat
and waited; through mist-filled daylight heard

the throbbing engine of a boat … All flesh, I thought,
is stone, is water … I had been, and would be

part of it, pain and prayer, rock and guano-white cliff-ledges;
would touch again the universal Christ,

the urgency, exemplar and the ground, Christ
the truth, the pity, and the truth.

Skellig

This is procession, across packed dirt,
the bodies, cowled, moving
to a stooping, apostolic, down-and-in

dampness of the oratory, procession
that goes on for ever,
high over the world in an embraced, embracing grief.

A process. Eucharist. Of mourning. Of rewriting
lives in a testament of rock.
Who are become priests of stone: this, too, my body—here,

my blood. Gannets amble on the air
in the surplice-white of body,
sacred black wing-tips, and suddenly a lance-dive down

until you know this, too, is slaughter, faster than stroke
or coronary, this the process, too, disturbing.
Fulmars soar from high-brow ledges, easy as sighing,

easy as prayer; the wind-honed, entrenched will,
love ultimately, over
(with a horror of height, and the midriff astrain ...)

soaring laud-birds and the far-below insistent
murmurous ocean. Through the feebleness
of faith, its febrile insistent sistings, process: half-moon

soft as a sucked host against the palate of the sky.
Where death, the stranger,
through a gritted taxing of the body, may become

a friend. You can hear them still, ascetics
who whisper amongst themselves,
amongst the glassworts and samphires, sisyphussing

up and down, death to life and back; and though the high
trail of a jet appears
unfamiliar, not one thing changed; it is the ongoing

ministrations of gravity and grace, of fall and lift, of doubt ... Un-
blink, erosions of the stone cross
are no longer visible, and the chipped nails of a strained monk

are still stained black by soil; the guttural muttering-together
of the fulmar—put ye on
the Lord Jesus—has not altered. Black today the face of the rock,

gulls, resting, are a language of their own in white chalk;
rock, knitted to rock, bonework
of the island, and its blood is Christ: and always green-blue water

offers its white petals, pouring cream down the eager
slopes of the boulders;
 the long back-drawing sigh, the hiss; a roiling of waters

and thin carpets of soiled foam float out; all this, you know it,
are spillings from the long
procession, bead-strings, small waltzings on the sunlit surfaces,

it is, amongst us all, communion, Christ-loss, absence,
the abandoned faith-yards
surviving where the chipped-off steps lean out over the sky.

I prayed, mountain-top, at the edge
of a shadow that could be God's; I knelt
on the bones of the earth while the bird of the fastnesses—

peregrinus—moved in its sacred spaces,
above me, within, without, the music of the winds
like an old plain chant. Suddenly I was home again,

while we knelt at dusk, our small
gravid family, to pray the rosary; I heard
the slow turning of the vowels and consonants, the sigh

of turves relaxing in the grate;
out in the centre of the room an oil-lamp
whispered out of its mantle, the flame through gauze

was yellow as honey-wax
but when the great night-moth
blundered in I heard a scream like the call of a soul in Hell;

by day, in school, we sat unslouched,
new tin whistles before us on the desks;
Brother had placed the charts against the wall, icons

of the language of doh-re-me, and finger
positions on the instruments; we would learn
Faith of our Fathers first, in C, *The Minstrel Boy*, later

in F. For the first minutes,
impatient with the scales and frustrated
by the necessities of technique, we made most wonderful

cacophonies. Soon, some of us
gave up, turning the whistles to pea-shooters, some
persisted, *We will be true to thee till death*. Tonight, on Skellig, I have loved

the ease of evening and embrace of night,
how the stars were taking, in silence, to their stations,
how the white ghosts of the butterflies tossed, all day,

their fragile lives in frenzy
into the arms of lavender and ladysmock,
and how *Faith of our Fathers* still grates sadly against the ear.

Theo Dorgan

Sailing to the Edge

1

A sail on the horizon,
make it two,
cloud pennant
at each truck;
(the rise and fall,
the south wind)
slow moving,
both hull down.

We tend ship,
haul fenders in,
coil dripping lines;
we settle
to the swell,
dispose ourselves,
seek shelter
from the wind.

I look again,
not sails but
island peaks,
deep-rooted
in deep water,
the tide sweeps
past their bows;
we slant off south.

Cormorants,
gannets, shags,
shearwaters,
petrels, gulls—
we make for
a cloud of souls
swept upward
into cloud.

2

Chug of the diesel, water slop in bilge.
The boatman throttles back a hint,
we dip to the swell. We settle.

Who made out first from Portmagee
for these black peaks, what hull
danced under him, what was in his mind?

For now I don't care, happy to be at sea,
braced to the lift and fall, at home out here.
I turn my phone off, unscrew the thermos, drink.

3

Province of sword and fire, of lust for land—
and that other province, of minds hungry for God,

for first and last things, far horizons.
One interweaved in the other, a riddle unpicked

when strong-minded abbots sailed
to build Christ's citadel on a rock.

Michael for patron, prince of angels, warrior saint.
An island fortress on the world's edge.

4

We land on the surge, the boatman wrestling the wheel,
the mass of rock looms over us, solid and black.

One element for another; mocked by the wheeling gulls,
we climb heavy-footed into air. Salt on my sleeve

when I pause to wipe my brow, shale & samphire at my feet.
Weight presses us from beneath, pushing through lungs,

opening us out until we stand clear on the North Peak.
Down there and out, and out again, the sea and the sea beyond.

Simple as that. We stoop and step inside, taking it all in—
the limestone pavement, the wells, the corbelled huts—

made thoughtful, of course, impressed, but also elsewhere.
The elsewhere that is eternal here and now.

5

Coptic or Greek or native Irish, what would it matter
to that black cormorant falling past like a thunderbolt?

The sun blazes out over far hills and valleys,
there in that other place beyond the sea

where fathers and mothers and homes are no more than dreams,
where a child, dreaming, sees two sails far out to sea.

The sun blazes on overhead although there's a storm coming—
the boatman earlier, tracking its advent, said
magicseaweed.com is the best of prophets—
the sun blazes down on us from the blank future,

circled by souls from the living past,
gleams on the wind, spume in our eyes.

6

We climb to the South Peak, privileged, on ropes,
belayed on each steep pitch, alive to danger,

and there on the high hermitage we turn to the west,
fearing to see God knows what. Beneath us, cliff edge,

a ledge of prayer. Monks would kneel here,
hands uplifted, for hours on end.

Fulmars and petrels barrel past, scanting the wind.
That ancient, light-packed trope—the soul as bird.

7

The swell's come up, the boat home edges in.
The black wall recedes in a wash of surf.

We heel, and then we're tide-borne, steady,
making out solid and sure for haven, home.

Layers of paint on the thwart, the wheelhouse, hot in the sun.
The chill comes on quickly as the wind picks up.

The cove opens its arms to us, we turn in,
butting the rising waves, the offshore chop.

The wind's come up, keening then deepening to a roar,
fading away until some remembered sorrow calls it back.

I feel it in my bones: tonight under the low cliff
will be growl and suck of surf, pounding,

the ground under the house shook—
the boatman knows, I catch it in his look.

Behind us the islands have turned north,
sailing into the wind now, wind of the coming storm.

Kerry Hardie

A High Tradition

At Cill Rialaigh Monastic Site

There are big slabs of whitish-grey rock in the fields and sheep lying about in the mist. The bombed-out foxglove stems stand up by the sides of the road like sentinels that no one's told the war's long over. Small droplets of rain cling to the barbed wire and the heather goes on blooming brightly, one of those plants that throws off moisture, though water clings with intricate precision to every flowering frond of the wild grasses.

The spider's webs are like spread nets catching the mist from the sky. The sheep hardly move—they might as well be stones or the stones might as well be sheep—and the edge of the fields falls off into a vacancy like deep, drugged sleep.

The road I walk should take me around the south slope of Bolus Head, where the remains of an early Christian monastic site lies somewhere off in the mist to my left. Or that's what it says in the book I am using.

> There [was] a monastery here, with a thick enclosure wall and an outer terrace; two upright stone slabs guard the outer entrance, and a church, cross-slabs, a souterrain and collapsed huts are within the inner enclosure.

The book—*The Modern Traveller to the Early Irish Church* by Ann Hamlin and Kathleen Hughes—also says that the view to the west includes Skellig Michael, but when I checked the contours on the map there seemed to be a headland in the way. It is a good book—scholarly, reliable. I strain my eyes, peering through vapour. Perhaps the authors came looking on a day like today, or perhaps there had been some other day when they'd climbed the steep slope to Bolus' height and seen the Skelligs afloat on a shining sea.

They do that. Appear and reappear—round a twist in the roads that wind these bays and headlands, round a twist in the mythic landscapes of the mind. They could easily have drifted in under the desklight when the notes for the book were being assembled; if Ann Hamlin had closed her eyes she might have stood once more on Cill Rialaigh's enclosure wall and seen Skellig Michael rising away to the west.

There's a scuffling off to my right and a gaggle of big bouncy lambs looms out of the mist. Fat and handsome they look, all fresh and white and fluffy; not long now till mid-season slaughter. They look at me looking at them and then vanish back to where they came from.

I give up using my eyes and try using my ears. No sound but the water run-offs and trickles, the sea now so far below the road that its distant shushing sound has fallen away. There's a stonechat up on a lump of rock, but even he's left off chatting. It's all so quiet I start thinking of Synge and his lonesome roads, I start thinking *like* Synge so the words are changing shape in my head and re-forming themselves into speeches from *Playboy* and maybe it's time to go back down the hill and buy a sandwich-bar wrap in Ballinskelligs, along with *The Irish Times* or *Kerry's Eye*—anything to halt all this regression.

I go on.

The Ascetics

I am sitting outside a cottage in the reconstructed village of Cill Rialaigh.

The morning is damp but visibility, though a bit smeary, has returned. Over the rise come the shouts of a man who is trying to get his dog to round up his sheep.

I am thinking about the idea of asceticism, and where it occurs in the Gospels, if at all. Everything coming to mind says the opposite. There is Christ making sure the drink lasts out the party, feeding crowds on loaves and fishes, refusing to condemn the prostitute, restoring the joy of the body by healing the sick. Certainly he seemed to own very little, but I can't remember much talk of deliberate starvation, and the time in the wilderness is shown as a time-of-trial, but not a trial-by-choice.

Yet the early church—in Ireland and elsewhere—revered the ascetic. Men and women who took themselves off to north African deserts or voluntarily starved and shivered on lumps of bare rock were held in the highest regard. The Celtic Church embraced the ideals of the Desert Fathers. Hermits and anchorites built oratories and cells; monastic enclosures were founded all down the Western shores of this island.

The mizzly rain has backed off now and the sun has just located itself behind thinning veils of cloud. The light is pale. The dog must be doing his stuff because the man has stopped yelling and there is some baaing and bleating. There's the crash of a metal gate swinging shut then an engine starts up and the sounds of a car die away. Cill Rialaigh village lies just down the road from the Cill Rialaigh monastic site I've been stumbling around in the mist. Though often refered to as a pre-famine village, it was emptied by emigration in the mid-twentieth century.

Asceticism again—or rather the refusal of asceticism: the young people turning away from a life that was just too hard. And some left urgently and without regret, while others lived the future haunted by the life they'd left.

A wind has risen from nowhere, rifling this notebook, blowing loose pages free so I have to run to retrieve them. Just as suddenly it dies, and I hear the drone of a bee. This is exactly what happens to me when I try and think about the monks on Skellig. One minute it's all a bluster of contradictions, and the next the wind drops, and there's only a solitary bee meandering about in the purple spikes of the loosestrife, sipping up nectar to turn into honey.

The Early Church

Kathleen Hughes has written eloquently on the place of the early monasteries in Irish society. She has explained their educational and religious contribution, outlined their function as places that offered a complex of services including fosterage, sanctuary for those fleeing their enemies, programmes of retribution for wrongdoers, and the provision of secure communal granaries in troubled times. No one can read her words and argue that monasteries in early Irish society did not earn their keep in worldly terms.

There is a Sufi story that is relevant at this point. It tells of a holy man (or Sheikh as they were—and still are—called) who lived in the trading district of a busy city and was visited by a messenger from another Sheikh who lived all alone on a mountain. The messenger delivered formal greetings, then announced his teacher's imminent arrival. The market-Sheikh was unimpressed by the news of the mountain-Sheikh's visit. It was easy enough to be holy on top of a mountain, he said; a man who lived on a mountain could disappear into contemplation of silence and space, he didn't have to live with the chance that the spice merchant's straying camel might land her full weight on his toe.

The Sheikh-who-lived-in-the-market had a point. Perhaps it was easier to be holy on Skellig Michael; perhaps if you were usually only partially in your body then you didn't fully notice that you were hungry and cold.

The discussion is really to do with the nature of mystical experience. Everyone knows that hunger and lack of sleep do something strange to the senses. Look at Lough Derg with its pilgrimage—everyone fasting and going without sleep. Look at Hemingway—that least ascetic of men—who wrote of the heightened perception he experienced just by going without his lunch in Paris when he was broke.

So am I suggesting that mystics see angels because they are hungry? Not quite. Mystics experience 'states' that are abnormal. Lots of 'normal' people do the same. Discuss abnormal states in a general way in any gathering and watch who gets a funny look on their face. Nine times out of ten that person has had some experience to do with something he afterwards feels around to describe and comes up with a word close to 'oneness'. But, like the Sheikh in the Sufi story, he lives in the market-place; perhaps he is even the vendor of spices whose camel has crushed the acknowledged mystic's toe. An abnormal state is abnormal, as he or she quickly discovers when he or she tries to explain the strange place where they suddenly found themselves on the way to collecting the kids from school or the car that was in for a service. So they learn to stay silent about the experience, but not to forget. The 'abnormal state' stays hidden inside them. Sometimes it's placed in some sort of shrine especially constructed to house it—a separate place, yet one that can be visited when the need is strong.

I suspect that mystics are just normal people who've had an abnormal experience and have chosen—for one reason or another—not to shut it away but to seek to explain it to themselves. In order to explain it they have to explore it, and in order to explore it they have to open themselves to its repetition.

Hence the pursuit of a life lived in isolated communities in the early church. Some of these communities must have been a lot less useful in worldly terms than those described by Kathleen Hughes at the start of this section, since they were often too poor, too introverted and too remote to fulfill most of the practical worldly functions she lists. But perhaps their role lay in providing for needs of a different order—needs not rational but mythic, not communal but individual; needs that are real yet without existence, like a sheet of light that lies on dark water after the rain has passed.

Solitude

Mystics have always liked mountains and deserts. It doesn't matter what tradition they're following, the pattern repeats and repeats. Whether they go hungry in order to increase the likelihood of entering an out-of-body state or whether the out-of-body state they are experiencing means they don't notice the body's need for food, the result is the same.

Solitude helps as well. Apart from anything else, it means your toe is less likely to get trampled. And though you may not suffer unduly while not entirely present, the pain will be there, waiting to kick in, as soon as you get back. Also solitude makes it easier to be present—which is a necessary preliminary to being absent. It is common knowledge that protracted periods of solitude lead (like Hemingway's empty belly) to a heightened awareness. Heightened awareness is not the same as an experience of oneness, but it's going in that direction. Spend several days entirely alone and notice how the world changes. It's as though the mind's breathing slows and you start to notice things you've passed over, things that were always there but that went unseen when the mind was busy. Your eye rests on a drystone wall and gets lost in the maze of the stones. It falls on a flower seen thousands of times and is stunned by its startling blueness. Everything in you has focused. Athletes call this 'entering the zone'. Mystics long to stay in the zone, to leave behind them the pain of absenting themselves from the place where they do not exist and yet where existence it total—the place where the blue flower's blueness enters the eye and saturates all with its beauty.

The Praise of the Natural World

There is a tradition of nature poetry in Irish literature that is claimed to be as ancient as the earliest stories. It is hard to separate out what is Christian and what is pagan because the pagan story-cycles and poems were mostly recorded in the scriptoriums of the early monasteries. In a sense, *separation* is not important, the point to note is how one has fed into the other, lending the later tradition some of the characteristics of the earlier one. The love of the natural world— of the white wave, the many-voiced birds, the dark lake, the belling stag—shines so clearly through both Christian prayer and pagan invocation that it is hard not to feel that both traditions experienced the world as the body of God. Perhaps Robin Flower, the scholar and translator, was observing this when he wrote the following words:

> It was not only that these scribes and anchorites lived by the destiny of their dedication in an environment of wood and sky and sea; it was because they brought into that environment an eye washed miraculously clear.

What washed the eye clear? What made them seek out lonely places of wood and sky and sea? Was it the search for God in the world or the search for God in themselves as part of the natural world?

The Island

Before my first visit to Skellig Michael I asked myself *why*. I felt there was something deeply unnatural in anchorites choosing to live on bare rock eight miles from the nearest inhabited land and practising such extreme mortification of the body. The idea of a quest for ecstatic experience never once crossed my mind.

The extraordinary lightness of spirit I felt when I stood on the island was the last thing I had anticipated. The sense of peace was equally unexpected.

The wind died inside me, the bee found the nectar and sipped.

The State

What is ecstatic experience? The books of all traditions describe it as 'union with God'—the experience of losing individual identity and being merged in a state of oneness and immortality that yet loves what is mortal.

The Miraculous

There is a sort of cheerful heartfelt simplicity about many of the Celtic saint-tales, and the miraculous is never a problem. Gifts are laid in reed baskets and sent down the Shannon to find their intended recipient; missals fall into deep pools and surface unmarked after years; pails full of water are turned into pails full of honey by holy children and used as fees for their schooling. The shamanistic world of animal-participation is deeply present. Stags lend their horns as book-rests for saints; blackbirds lay eggs in a saint's outstretched hand; whales rise from the sea, offering their backs as dry land for the celebration of the Easter mass. There are voyage tales, magic spells, prophesies of the births of marvellous children who will become marvellous men. In Celtic Christianity saints are mostly born, not made.

So did the men who chose to live out their lives on Skellig Michael care about sainthood? Or did they go there to enter so deeply into themselves that they lost themselves and belonged to the world instead?

Those little magical tales of mice nibbling the ears of Mo Chua to wake him for office, of sea-otters bringing firewood and fish to Paul on his island; of stags carrying loads of cut wood for Finian— are they just quaint embellishments or did they symbolise a deep state of harmony with the natural world?

Distance

From Cill Rialaigh, even when the day is fine, you cannot see Skellig Michael. Cill Rialaigh looks south to Scariff Island, with the smaller island of Deenish tucked in in its lee. Behind these islands you can see the long promontory of the Beara Peninsula. Mountainous and sinewy, it stretches along a horizon that's further broken by small rocky outcrops and islands. On soft days of low cloud and small winds, the Beara Penisula unhinges itself from the mainland and floats. The horizon is ghosted with islands.

There isn't much left of the monastery of Cill Rialaigh. There's a massive enclosing wall and within it the remains of a tiny oratory, a souterrain and the ruins of beehive huts. A cross-marked stone slab still stands in the *leacht* or graveyard; another leans by the oratory's remains.

Cross over the headland of Bolus between the lower shoulder of Canuig Mountain and Knocknashereighta and join the road that follows the pass then opens and drops to the sea. The view changes with such abruptness it's hard not to brake and stop dead. Below you the whole wide expanse of St. Finian's Bay opens and stretches off to Eternity, with America somewhere beyond. You will hardly bother with it. Instead you will stare at the rough, leaning cone of rock that rises sheer from the sea. In fact it isn't a cone at all, but two islands—Little Skellig and Skellig Michael. From this angle the smaller island is seen against its larger neighbour. The eye sees just one mythic island afloat in a mythic sea

The road here bends north, then turns west in a dog's-leg curve. Just past the dog's leg you can leave the road and climb to the substantial early Christian monastic site of Killabuonia. The oratory faces north east. From its all-but overgrown southwestern entrance you'll see Skellig Michael. Was it built here for this reason? Did its monks look in longing at the peak of St. Michael's ascetics, or thank their maker that eight miles of open sea lay between his cell and theirs?

Which brings us back to Sheikhs who live in the markets and their brothers who inhabit mountains.

Despite the isolation of their island eyrie, the monks felt the need of a place of further retreat. Tucked around the back of the South Peak of Skellig Michael there is a hermitage. Off the path on the arduous climb up to that hermitage, human hands have constructed a platform that projects from the side of the mountain and falls sheer on three sides to the sea. It faces west, is ringed by a low wall and lined with quartz, the stone used on sacred sites since time began. Kneel on this platform and the wall blocks peripheral vision. You see only a vast infinity and a faint line where the sea meets the sky. It's not hard to imagine the men who knelt there experiencing union with something both finite and infinite.

The Choice

But what of those market-sheikhs, the men who inhabited Cill Rialaigh? Not much of a market-place, you might say, not exactly crowded with camels and spice-merchants. Not so extensive either, just an oratory tucked in under an enclosing wall and a few dry-stone huts, built from rough stone, for dwellings. But these shoreline monasteries were also ascetic, they also housed small groups of men whose pursuit was mystical practice. With one enormous difference. They lived on the mainland and not on that mountain; they were accessible; their devotion to asceticism was a daily choice; they had to interact with the society in which they dwelled.

So which was the superior way?

The market place or the mountain?

The Beginnings

St. Patrick was a magus. In the *Tripartite Life of Patrick* and *The Lebar Brecc Homily on St. Patrick* he mounts a hero's assault on Tara, and then, in a series of supernatural contests, forces the king to conversion, and deals such a mortal blow to the ancient tradition that it never recovers its former prestige and power. There's no gentle pastoral here. Like deals with like, and Patrick emerges a mighty wizard, a kingly priest and a prophet of awesome prowess. The action on both sides is dark and raw and about as gentle as an eagle's talons ripping the flesh from new lambs.

But St. Patrick's *Confessio*—allegedly written in his own hand—comes out of a tradition so different to this account that it reminds of the stirring of leaves on a summer's night in a balmy, southerly land:

> I saw in a vision of the night a man whose name was Victorius coming as it were from Ireland with countless letters. He gave me one of them, and I read the beginning of the letter, which was entitled 'The Voice of the Irish.' And whilst I was reading aloud the beginning of the letter I thought that at that very moment I heard the voices of those who dwelt beside the Wood of Foclut, which is nigh unto the Western Sea. And thus they cried, as with one mouth, 'We beseech thee, holy youth, to come and walk once more amongst us.'

It is widely accepted that this *Confessio* is the document that reflects the authentic tone of Patricius the Roman, though it may well, like the *Tripartite Life*, have passed through the hands of many scribes. Who knows how much its sweet tone of reason is owed to their pens?

But it throws up a question it's hard not to ask. How could the 'holy youth' revealed by this text have bested the Druids, converted the High King, and evangelised so extensively and with such improbable success, unless he was a 'man of power' in the Shamanic sense, as well as a Christian priest?

There are versions of all stories, all stories have versions, there is no such thing as the last word, and even the camera is not a reliable witness.

Sacrifice

> When Columb Cille reached the place that today is called 'Hi of Columb Cille' [Iona], he said to his household: "It is well for us that our roots should go underground here." And he said: "It is permitted to you that some one of you should go under the earth here or under the mould of the island to consecrate it." Odran rose up readily, and this he said: "If I should be taken," saith he, "I am ready for that." Saith Columb Cille: "O Odran! Thou shalt have the reward thereof. No prayer shall be granted to anyone at my grave unless it is first asked of thee." Then Odran went to heaven. Saint Columb founded a church.
> — *'The Lives of the Saints'*, *The Book of Lismore*

The monks in the monasteries recorded the old pagan stories as well as the old Christian stories. Voluntary sacrifice on behalf of the wider community (reward to be granted in heaven) is as old as those strangled corpses dug out of ancient bogs, or the monks' skulls buried under the corner-posts of Tibetan monasteries. And as recent as the shrine to the suicide bomber.

Shamanism, and the indentification of God with the natural world, are also traditions as old as humankind's need to worship.

The question is this: did the old stories bleed into the scribes' accounts, or did the old ways bleed into early Christian practice?

Are sacrifice and asceticism as old as humanity and, though hidden to what we now call the 'rational mind', so necessary that they will find their way into some aspect of every code of beliefs that humanity devises?

Whether or not they were central to the life (as opposed to the death) of the being called Jesus is still open to debate.

Around Me

It is mid-August. The wild grasses rise blanched and sere, the loosestrife makes purple spikes in the boggy ground, a veiled sun throws long lines of muted light on the unquiet sea.

Relocation

Nobody knows why the monks left Skellig Michael for Ballinskelligs, nor when the Augustinian rule was adopted in the new abbey; nobody knows when the new abbey, in its turn, closed its doors, nor the definitive fate of its monks, though there are theories. For hundreds of years there were men and women, unlettered in English, who lived round these coasts and gathered the stories the people had told down the ages, and the stories go back and back to pre-history. So why has so little history of the church survived?

The anchorite monks left the island and no one knows the cause. Perhaps a drop of a few degrees in the climate, perhaps a fall-off of young men drawn to a life on a mountainy rock in the sea.

Besides, there was change in the air. The abbots were losing their power to the bishops, the autonomous monasteries of the Celtic church were being displaced or replaced by the great continental orders that spread across Ireland from the 12th century onwards. Whatever the way of it was, the Augustinians were unlikely to have been empathetic successors to the Skellig anchorites. Disputes there may well have been between sheikhs of the mountain and sheikhs of the market place, but the Augustinians—highly trained, talented administrators, deeply committed to the implementation of doctrinal orthodoxy—were closer to Mullahs ensconced in the mosque than the holy men and women who made it as anchorites or saints or sheikhs.

The abbey that replaced Skellig Michael lies on the shores of Ballinskelligs Bay. The bay sweeps round in a great curving arc but the abbey is sited in the lee of the old McCarthy stronghold, a logical precaution given the unquiet times. Logical, and yet there is something very curious about this siting. Walk its bounds and you'll look in vain for a view of the open sea. Everywhere that there's a break in the land, an island floats just further out, blocking the eye's free passage. The abbey has been moved from its perch on an eyrie surrounded by sea to a sheltered site on a bay apparently encircled by land.

People come from all over the world to visit Skellig Michael, sometimes making the journey over and over, awaiting the time that the weather will quiet enough for a landing.

No one visits the other Abbey, the one encircled by islands and headlands; they want the monastery in the sky, entirely encircled by water. They climb from the bobbing boats and stand at the foot of the steps and ready themselves for the long climb up the ancient steps to the saddle. A few—like the Orthodox monk described in Paddy Bushe's fine poem, *Lohar*—understand what they're coming to. ("It was simply, he smiled / A *peregrinatio pro Christi*".) Most of us don't—or not till after we've descended the steps, reboarded the boats and made the long trip home to to our everyday lives. But once you have been on the island it never leaves you.

It is 800 years since the monks left the rock, but the beehive huts and the small stone oratories still speak down the years of a lost, high tradition a few, extraordinary men once trod.

> Look you out
> northeastwards
> over mighty ocean,

teeming with sea-life;
home of seals,
sporting, splendid,
its tide has reached
fullness.

Translated from the Old Irish by James Carney

Reading Heinrich Boll's *The Clown* on a bus bound for Skellig Michael

In Waterford they've taken the first cut.
The Friesians lie in grass like malachite.
The elder's fresh in flower but the bus windows
are double-glazed against its heavy scent.

I'm envying this character in the book I'm reading,
who picks up smells through glass, or down the phone.
We pass a meadow where they're tossing hay—
a drowning fragrance like a summer sea.

He's some class of clown, this vagrant smell-man,
working the German stage after the war,
sending mimed bullets out into the audience,
his life a leaden place of blank despair.

I'll take him with me to the ghosts on *Sceilg*
who fast and chant above their ink-dark seas.
They won't mind him as he's not a joiner;
he can't stand dogma though he's close to God.

He'll have the puffins for clown-comrades
crowding the steps-to-heaven in the dusk,
nor will he shirk the climb, this theatre athlete,
for every step he will loosen his bound life.

He'll walk through their stone gates with nothing,
then lie down on the place of graves and sigh
because at last he will have found some absence,
and in the sea-light will be space to die.

Skellig Michael

Wind hones their crosses cut from standing rocks—
stone blades that slice the sunlight, slice the sky.
Weather nips and worries at their walls
that dogged hands re-sculpted against storm.

I've searched for them in texts,
pored over colour plates of books and bells,
of reliquaries for arm-bones, girdles, teeth.
They left no artefacts, no shrines.

What need had they of such?
They were the shrine.
The pattern and the pilgrimage.
The way.

Sky Station

Who kneels on the quartz
watching the place
where the sea meets the sky?

Who has the body that's cold in the wind
that blows from the place
where the sea meets the sky?

Who is it who worships,
who is it who's worshipped,
but he-who-is god,

praising god?

Strange Company

Someone moved my hands into known holds carved in the rock.
Someone eased my feet into the pocks.
Someone's laughter bubbled in my throat.
Someone's fearlessness erased my fear.

No one climbed the cliff. No one descended.
Everything was as it was, would always be.
Infinity laid out in wind and stone.
The ancient Rule: the wind undoes, the stone defies.

There was a platform, a sea-eagle's rake.
A seam chipped in bare rock to channel rain.
A ledge that straddled space, creating place.
Blue sheepsbit scabious in the sandy grit.

Someone used my eyes to look.
Someone used my heart to soar.
No one spoke to me of death.
Death belongs with time and time was not.

Biddy Jenkinson

Bun na Faille

Pulcann uain farraige san uaimh chaol.
Pléascann.

Bheadh níos mó iontaoibhe agam
as an gcloigeann daonna
dá mbeadh leithead ann
nó slí as.

Smál

Déanadh cuileoga
de dhroch smaointe
na manach.

Shíolraigh siad.

Clochán

Idir an ghile amuigh
agus an manach sa dorchadas istigh,
tá snáth síoda amháin
feadh an dorais
agus dathanna an tsaoil
ag imirt ann.

Suí Fhionan

Arsa Fionan le Finín
'Déanaimís an splinc a leacú
agus clochar a thógáil air
chun onóra Dé.'

Arsa Finín le Fionan,
'Fágtar an splinc
don Té a thuirlingeos air.
Tógtar cillín
faoina scáil.'

An Ceangal
Is a cháirde na páirte, tuigtear gur caoch an cheist í:
'Cad chuige gur thóg siad laftán thuas ansin
as ucht Dé?'
Nuair nach bhfuil freagra le fáil ach gur thíos seachas thuas tá an lios
is an stairricín carraige maol ina chloch phréacháin ag mac Dé.

Sólás

'San doineann, a bhráithre,
gluaiseann an Sceilg go seolta
trín gceo
i leith na síoraíochta.

Sa tsoineann,
titeann sí
i dtrapaisí.'

An Manach agus an Chailleach Nite Éadaigh

San ardthráthnóna
thit Donnchadh Bán le faill
agus cailleadh é.

Bhí strapa á thógáil aige ag an am.

Athmhaidin an lae úd
chonaic sé cailleach
agus léine fola á ní aici
sa taoide.

Chuir sé lámh laistigh dá chóta
féachaint an mbeadh a léine air
i gcónaí,
agus bhí.

'Cé leis an léine, a bhean chóir?'
ar seisean, de bhéic, leis an gcailleach.
'Leis an Sceilg,' ar sise.
'Léine in aghaidh na bliana,
cuid na carraige.'

D'fhill Donnchadh ar a chuid oibre
agus lean an chailleach
ag tomadh agus ag tarraingt
an éadaigh trín uisce,
mar a dhéanfadh bean tí mhaith ar bith.

Brionglóid Sceilge

Ba mise mé féin
Naomh Lomán
im shuí sa tsáile
—mo cheann ris—
gur fhás giúrainn orm.

Bhí orm dreapadh
asam féin ansin
agus suí
im fhaoisceán
ar mo ghogaidí,
ar mo chloigeann,
go bhfaighinn cóiriú
ón ngaoth aduaidh
go mbeadh an tonn
oigheartha go leor
le go bhfaighinn
fuar arís é.
Agus fuair.

D'fhéachas síos uaim
ar ball beag
féachaint an rabhas
ceangailte dem mhuineál fós
nó ná rabhas.

Bhí ina lán mhara
agus bhí a gcrobha amuigh
ag mo chuid giúrann uilig,
agus iad ag scagadh bídh
ón ngoirme,
sa chaoi is go rabhas clúdaithe
le tuíneach

de chleití farraige
im fhile dílis

Agus reiceas
in ard mo ghutha
dán
a thuig giúrainn
agus faoileáin.

Limistéir

In Éirinn
bíonn imlíne ar an dán.
Anseo, an dán an t-imlíne.

Ar eagla mo chaillte
bogaim báirneach den leac
agus suím ina áit
ag iníor.

The Last Holy Woman of Sceilg

The wind veered southwest in the night. Though the sea heaved mightily, the waves, no longer confused, came in rhythmic surges. Bric and Colmán climbed to Suí Fhionan, as soon as the day cleared, to look out for Maoilín, the *naomhóg* that had gone to the mainland to bring Christmas supplies home to Sceilg.

Their seniors, Dá, Berrach and Lugh, knowing that two of the three rowers had attained the use of reason, gathered in the large *cillín* that served as kitchen, living area, scriptorium, infirmary. They offered thanks for what they were about to receive, whenever Maoilín arrived, and began the hour's appointed task: shelling hazelnuts.

Three sods of turf, smouldering in a large iron pot, contributed smoke.

'What's that?' Bric, poised where the Norman St. Michael would descend six centuries later, pointed to an object west of Splinc an Bhodaigh, that gathered the dim light of the morning to itself and rode the waves lightly.

'Dead white seal.'

'No. Too lively. I'm going down to see ...'

Bric flew down the cliff face. He hadn't walked on level ground since his stint on the out-farm on Dairbhre during the harvest, so vertical had become as horizontal. Colmán followed him. By the time they reached the splinc the swell had carried the white seal past the *cuasán* and an eddy had caught it.

'I'll get it before it shifts.'

Only a direct order from Berrach would stop him.

'Put that around you.'

Colmán handed him the horsehair rope used to tie Maoilín in fine weather.

Bric launched himself. The sea played tricks, as she must, but eventually she yielded the white seal to Bric and slacked her grip on him sufficiently to allow Colmán to pull him in, clutching his prize. They hauled the object higher and squatted beside it.

'It's a skin bottle.'
'A boat-shaped bottle?'
'Why not?'
The bottle trembled.
'Chríost!'
Colmán took his knife, slit the skin carefully and revealed a baby's head.
'Mermaid's purse! A mermaid's child.'
Colmán took the purse under his arm. Bric skirted up his sopping *seanóg* and they raced to the Cill to show their find to Berrach.

Berrach, Dá and Lugh looked up from the task in hand. Berrach swept the nuts aside to make space on the table for the prize that the youngsters had lugged in without remembering to pray *Dia anseo isteach!*

Shaking—it must have been with excitement, for salt water is never truly cold off the blessed Sceilg—Bric displayed his find. The blue eyes were open and staring, the face white and composed, a suggestion of gold above the eyes and at the temples.

'It can't be dead. It moved ....'

A fist came out of the wrappings and found the mouth which opened. The face screwed into a horrid purple parody of itself. Another fist appeared and boxed the mouth. The noise began. Colmán and Lugh blessed themselves.

'The child is hungry,' said Dá. He lifted it from its shell with the authority of experience. He had fathered ten children before leaving *cetmuintir* (first wife), *ben tánaisteach* (second wife), and *adhaltrach* (concubine) many years before, for the glory of God and a *cillín* on Sceilg.

A human stink rose from the screeching bundle. A foot escaped and kicked away the mermaid.

'Colmán! Liven the fire. Boil water. Has anyone a clean second *léine?*'

Lugh went to fetch his. Colmán opened the heart of the fire, added brosna and a fresh sod, coaxed it to life with his breath. Dá growled *'Dia do bheatha, a rí na n-aingeal...'*[1] hugging and rocking the bundle. He offered a little finger dipped in honey. The immediate silence drew the rest to gaze at the infant as it sucked with devout concentration.

Dá loosed the outer wrapping: *bannlámh* after *bannlámh* of cobweb-fine white stuff, touched here and there with gold.

'It is the *caille* of a queen,' exclaimed Bric.

Inside it there was a fleece of shorn wool.

'The bottom of it is like a sheep's tail in August,' said Colmán, who saw things as they were.

'Make fast-day gruel, Colmán. Add an iota each of butter and honey.'

'It is about three months old, Mo Bherrach [2]. We should be able to keep it alive.'

Berrach (who would have been abbot, had the hermits evolved into monks at the time in question), mindful of the dignity of seniority, drew away.

'Stand back!' Dá said, laughing. 'It isn't male.'

'A female!' Berrach startled.

'Well, it isn't a fish,' said Dá.

'And it was only a chance that I went in after it. Only a chance' said Bric, tears running down his face.

'God's will,' said Berrach.

'Colmán! Warm water and soap in the larger vessel. Get rags from the pen box.'

'Let Dá mind the child, since he is skilled. Let the rest of us consider,' said Berrach and he drew the long piece of shining white material through ring of thumb and index finger. 'It is *sról.*'

'Torn,' said Lugh.

The veil stretched from one hand to another and brought brightness into the *cillín*.

'Bless the craftsman,' said Berrach, examining the leather vessel that had contained the child. 'Fine seams. Beautifully waterproofed.

1. A hymn: Hail king* of angels ... (Christ*, not Michael)
2. Mo- before a name indicates venerability. In later times Berrach would be Ab or Abbot. Mo in placenames; Cill mo Choda—the Cill of Mo Choda—Kilmacud.

Weighted at the bottom. This small patch the size of a *screapall*, here, just beneath where the head lay, rubbed thin to let a little air in.'

'What monster would put a child to sea in that?' asked Bric, horrified.

'This is a *scrín*,' said Berrach. 'The child is a child of incest ...'

The word crashed on their souls, a drowning wave.

'... put in a *scrín* and placed in the sea where a white shield is no longer visible from the land, to live or die as God decides.'

'God had nothing to do with this,' snarled Dá.

'If it has pleased God to deliver the child to us, it is our responsibility,' said Berrach. 'If God had nothing to do with it, then we may have nothing to do with it, Dá, if we observe the new rules you wish on us.'

'Colmán, bring these to Berrach,' said Dá in a controlled voice. 'They were in a *tiachóg,* over the heart.'

Berrach drew out a piece of vellum and unwrapped a gold ring, not a simple open ring used for currency but one of intricate design.

'Read what is on the vellum, Bric.'

Bric brought it to the door and read:

'Muireann a h ainm.
Deirfiúr Mhuirchú
Ghrá a máthar
Nár chiontaigh.'[3]

'A woman's hand, made clear and bold for legibility. Has the child any imperfections, Dá?'

'A bad temper.'

'I am thinking of Lughaidh Ríamh Dhearg, whose body bore three red stripes in token of triple incest,' said Berrach.

'No red stripes. Many ordinary, small, light bruises and this great livid one that girdles the body.'

Berrach fingered the torn *caille.*

'Her mother held tight, but the ruthless hands won. Lugh, can you tell where the *scrín* came from?'

Lugh, who had travelled with Brendan, said:

3. *Her name is Muireann, sister of Muirchú, love of her mother, who didn't sin.*

'The *scrín* hasn't been in the sea for more than one night, or, tight as it is, it would have taken water. It rode high.'

'She came in from the south west,' said Colmán. 'Either she came from *tír tairngre* or …'

'Yesterday the wind was from the east. She was put out yesterday not far from here and was turned back by the changing wind. When did the wind change? I slept.'

'Early in the night.'

'Then the return took longer than the outward journey or she would have passed us by. Or else she was put in where an eastern current worked with the wind at the beginning.'

'Dairbhre! Everyone knows that the current off Dairbhre rushes eastward.'

'Perhaps. Maybe from Ceann Bhóluis …'

Dá had swaddled the baby in a *léine* and joined the cogitators while spooning honeyed water into the anxious mouth, scooping up the dribbles and returning them.

'But there is no one on Dairbhre or Bólus who could afford *sról* and gold. Our *rí tuaithe* has no female relations young enough to be sinned with fruitfully.

'The minds that fashioned this child's destiny were as contrary as the recent winds. From the mother, the fleece, the *caille,* the ring, the message, the light bruises of desperation, the *scrín,* seaworthy as the finest craftsman could make it. Opposed is a mind determined to kill by legal means.'

'A devout soul, scandalised by the nature of the sin and obeying the letter of the law,' suggested Lugh.

'No!' said Berrach decisively. 'Many have been put to sea on a sheltered strand when there was an inshore wind and a rising tide and mist would make the shield invisible at a few paces. This child is three months old. Someone waited until the wind came from the east and picked a place where the current would bring her past all hope of landing.'

'Nobody, within several days' travel, could have borne her, or we would have heard.'

'Why didn't the mother write down where she came from and

of what kin she was?'

'Fear for the child. Safer, should she live, that she be Muireann, the seaborn, and nothing else.'

'Berrach, though we can prevent starvation, the child needs its mother, or a wet nurse. It was taken from the breast. There is a little sucking blister on the upper lip.'

Bric and Colmán exchanged glances.

'With your blessing, Berrach, we will go to Ireland and find her mother. Tell us who she is and where we can find her.'

Dá held his breath.

'In a good cause …' murmured Lugh.

Berrach shook his head.

'*Imbas forosna* [4] is forbidden to a Christian.'

'*Gach reacht go h-éigean.*' [5]

'It will not be necessary to break the law. The mind can find an answer. Think! Reason! Deduce! Who would take trouble to drown a baby girl? We haven't got rabid holy men and lawyers in Mumhan who would seek out a small child to expose her. The deed was done within a *fine* and the law nodded. If there was incest, it was the excuse, not the cause. Greed used law and religion as its agents.'

'A question of inheritance?'

'You forget she is a girl.'

Berrach had been turning the ring on his index finger.

'The ring has a groove on one side. It is a half ring, the female half. The male half is missing. If I am right, there is another scrín out there with Muirchú, the male twin inside it. This one had to share his fate, for appearances sake.'

※

Bric moved towards the door before looking back for approval.

'Go with him, Colmán. Pray, Bric! But don't expect too much of the sea. This child is today's generosity.'

Dá tried thin sweet gruel on a small horn spatula and it was

---

4. *A form of druidic divination*   5. *A law holds till necessity intervenes*

accepted with much snorting and blowing. Berrach began to shell more hazels and Lugh to crush the kernels.

'Can you tell, Dá, how much time she spent in the *scrín*, both in the sea and before being set adrift?'

'Not by her deposits, since she hasn't been feeding. She is thirsty, but not desiccated. You think she went into the sea yesterday. When, Lugh?'

'Early enough to allow the shield to be seen.'

'Yes, the letter of the law would have been observed,' said Berrach, sadly.

'In the sea by mid afternoon. Put in the *scrín* not before the small hours of the morning.'

'Put in the *scrín* by a friend. The final seam is as the early ones. Then she was taken overland or over sea for nine hours before being floated at a selected place.'

'Nine hours' distance. We must know her people. Think!'

They thought. The child, temporarily fulfilled, looked at them and seemed to smile.

'*Is táth gach tátal,*'[6] said Berrach, 'but we must do the best we can with reason and imagination. If we are correct in our considerations, a woman gave birth to twins three months ago. She is skilled in writing, had enough wealth and influence to have this *scrín* constructed. She is without the protection of husband or father. She claims innocence and, though it is a woman's claim, it could be argued that it is of the nature of the oath of a dying woman at childbirth and admissible, if only in our deductions. If she is innocent, there was a husband. If the husband was a good man, he is dead. They were both people of substance, since wealth marries wealth. His death would have been a matter of record. Who, of note, died a year ago?'

'Can you ask that when a man of the Corca Laoighde is present, Berrach?' snapped Lugh. 'Have you forgotten our struggle against the Eoghnachta at Cnocán a Lingeáin in the spring?'

'The Corca Laoighde fought bravely in defence of their territory and lost many to the Eoghnachta. Ailbhe Ceanndearg, *ruirí* of the Laoighde of Ráth Ludhach, died in battle,' said Berrach placidly.

6. *Wispy every prognosis: all deduction is dodgy.*

'Who has replaced him?'
'His brother Donn.'
'Properly elected?'
'Yes.'
'Was there a son to inherit Ailbhe's property?'
'No. Ailbhe went to war from the marriage feast.'
'His bride?'
'Returned to her own people. She was a poet, only child of Conraí Caol the *ollamh,* who treated her as a son.'
'Why didn't they marry her to Ailbhe's brother and successor, Donn?'
'Never marry a female poet,' said Dá. The baby had turned its head into his breast and fallen asleep. 'They are opinionated persons, liable to satirise one and capable of inflicting incapacities.'
'There was also the matter of Donn's three existing wives,' said Lugh. 'He needs the approval of the Church. He was never popular with the *fine.* They elected Ailbhe, though Donn is older.'
'So the bride was sent home to her father, Conraí Caol,' said Berrach gently.
'Her lament for Ailbhe is well known. The poet who carried news of our defeat to Baile na Scealg sang a lament that she had composed.'
'Is her name known?'
'Íde.'
'Then this is Muireann, iníon Íde,' said Berrach, nodding at the baby. 'A wedding lasts seven days. Long enough to make a child.'
'You are mistaken, Berrach,' said Lugh. 'If this child is three months old, she was conceived at least a month and a half after Ailbhe's death.'
'That was one claim against her.' Berrach sat with his elbows among the nuts and his palms clasped to his cheeks and a distant look in his eyes. 'I see a girl putting her grief in a poem and returning to her father's house. She goes on circuit with him. What is there left to tie her to one place, rather than another? She finds that she is with child. Unwelcome news to those who have inherited Ailbhe's wealth and authority. They comfort themselves: it may be a girl. If a boy, it may not be Ailbhe's. Less than eight months after his death she bears twins. She takes Ailbhe's

1. Sunrise at the Wailing Woman
2. Little Skellig from below the Wailing Woman

3: Near the South Landing
4: Eoin Walsh's boat approaches the landing — in thankfully calm waters

5: *"... where the chipped-off steps lean out over the sky"* — 'Skellig', John F. Deane
6: Poet/editor Paddy Bushe before beginning the steep ascent

7: The disused lighthouse
8: The lighthouse children's grave in St. Michael's Church, a late medieval ruin in the monastic enclosure

9: The modern lighthouse seen from near the South Peak
10 (inset): Lighthouseman Raymond Wickham

11: The communal cell
12: Just about visible, a cross carved from a natural outcrop of rock

13: The monastery terrace. Like any other level ground on the island, the terrace is man-made, perched some 150 m. above sea-level. Before the monks, and subsequently the lighthouse men, hewed out their habitations, the island was as inhospitable and as inaccessible as Little Skellig, almost a mile away in the background.

14:
John F. Deane

15:
Biddy Jenkinson

16: The outer section of the monastery. The monastery seen by today's visitor is a culmination of centuries of collapse and rebuilding, layered one on top of the other. The structure in this photograph may be the earlist extant cell, located between the outer wall of the citadel and the inner monastic wall.

17: In the OPW hut, three poets — and a photographer!

18: Evening at the monastery, looking eastward towards the mainland.

19: Guarding the entrance. The herring gull is just one of the enormous number of species of marine birds (as well as visitors from the mainland) to be seen on both islands. Puffins and gannets are perhaps the most emblematic, although the gannets (more than 50,000 of them) confine themselves to Little Skellig.

20: Meditation terrace. A stunning, visionary location where, from a kneeling or sitting position, only the sea and the sky are visible.

21: The monastery terrace, looking westward

22: Theo Dorgan surveys the horizon

23: The monastery cemetery

24: Small oratory terrace, with oratory, leacht (shrine), cross and necessarium (toilet)

25: Layered entrance

26: The South Peak. After a hazardous traverse, and a vertical climb through The Eye of the Needle on the far side, the hermitage just below the peak is reached.

27: Looking westward from the South Landing. This is what the first monks would have been faced with.

28: John Minihan takes a break and lets somebody else manage the camera for a while. (Photograph by Paddy Bushe.)

children to Ailbhe's kin. Unwise decision. A case is made out against her. Perhaps it is made in good faith, though powered by particular interest. It is done through the judiciary: she has had time to have the *scrín* made.'

'It is not unknown for a child born at eight months, or even earlier, to survive,' said Dá.

'A cow with twin calves will often drop them before time,' said Lugh. "Excessive distention provokes contraction," is a maxim of the *cnáimhsigh*.[7] If this is a daughter of Ailbhe … If a son of his survives …'

'Lugh, where does Conraí Caol live?' Dá asked.

'Dúilios.'

'Then the child's mother is there.'

'Íde isn't there. She is in Ráth Lughach. Under restraint, held by Donn,' Berrach said with certainty.

'Unless she is dead or has become a nun,' said Dá soothing the baby's head as it shuddered in sleep.

'Berrach, do you see this, or are you guessing?'

Berrach startled and frowned.

'Of my own volition, I did nothing except cogitate. Yet I know that she lives and is bleeding for her babies.'

After that silence fell in the cillín. The child slept. There were no more nuts to shell.

༇

Colmán and Bric came back despondent. There was no sign of another *scrín*.

'Perhaps there was none,' said Berrach. 'Sometimes the thing imagined impresses the mind excessively and takes too definite a shape.'

'Berrach has deduced that the child Muireann is the daughter of Íde, daughter of Conraí Caol and that she is being held in Rath Lughach,' said Dá.

'Muireann is related to me,' proclaimed Lugh.

'The swell is less,' said Bric. 'Maoilín will return before night. Allow us to go and find the mother and bring her here, Berrach.'

---

7. Boners—*when it was necessary to break the pelvis to facilitate birth the early obstetrician was the 'boner'. The name Bonner is a relic of this profession.*

Jenkinson ༇ 97

Berrach did not reply. His face abstracted, his eyes distant, his elbows again among the hazels, his palms cradling his cheeks he said softly: 'Let there be a *cillín* built apart from the rest, yet within range of their protection.'

The adventures of Colmán, Bric, Lugh and Cormac who set out in the early morning in Maoilín and rescued Íde from under the noses of Donn's warriors, have been reported in Annála Úibh Ráthaigh. They brought Íde[8] safely to sanctuary on Sceilg, though pursued by the Corca Laoighde.[9] Íde never recovered the use of her left arm. Confident of her virtue she had submitted to *fír coiri*,[10] and plunged her arm into a boiling cauldron to take a pebble from the bottom, before the assembled accusers. Her arm had been scalded beyond curing. Guilty, as charged. The fact that she had exposed her left arm to the ordeal, when everyone knew that she wrote with her right, was considered a further proof of guilt.

Berrach called on knowledge that he had renounced to heal the broken and suppurating flesh and did penance for a year in expiation. Muireann thrived.

It is not known if Muirchú perished after being set adrift but there is an entry in the Annals to the effect that Donn Ceanndearg of the Corca Laoighde died at the hands of Muirchú, a *mac raite*[11] of Eoghnán of the Eoghanacht of Inis Neacail.

Dá no longer tried to convert his brother hermits to a more regular monastic life. It was not until after Íde's death that ties between the Sceilg and the foundation at Baile na Scealg strengthened and Sceilg itself was eventually abandoned.

The remains of a child were found on the Sceilg during excavations.

---

8. *Íde eventually acquired the 'mo' of veneration and is now better known as Míde.*
9. *It has been claimed that the crews of these boats served their Rí tuaithe badly on that day, possible by design, and that the insults hurled at them by Lugh had the effect of boiling oil.*
10. *The truth of the cauldron*
11. *Adopted son*

Glossary

Maoilín: name of a cow without horns. The naomhóg was called after the cow that had contributed the first hide.
naomhóg: boat, from Latin 'navis', a ship.
cillín: cell
splinc: pinnacle
cuas-cuasán: one of the larger indentations in the steep cliffs along the sea shore
seanóg: hooded cloak
Dia anseo isteach! Bless all here!
bannlámh: 21 inches
caille: veil
sról: silk
screapall: coin
scrín: shrine
tiachóg: small purse
tír tairngire: the land of promise
rí tuaithe: local king
Muireann (Muir ghin): sea born
Imbas forosna: a form of druidic divination. After chewing a piece of raw flesh, the druid puts his palms on his cheeks and is entranced. It is to be presumed that Berrach had training, as a druid, before his conversion.
ruirí: overking
ollamh: chief poet
fine: a tribal group

An Cat Mara

Manaigh a bhí ag dul go dtí An Caladh
fómhar na bliana 601 ach gur éirigh stoirm

An fharraige ina suan
nuair d'fhágamar an Sceilg.
An mhuir in aon bharr solais,
an Riabhach as radharc san aibhéis.

Sceilig na nÉan sciathánach,
an domhain tréshoilseach glas fúinn,
Carraig Lomáin, go heisceachtúil
gan lása faoina muineál.

Ach dhúisigh Pangar Dubh.
Léim a scáth ón ngrineall.
Chuir sé cruit air féin:
cham an léinseach ina coire.

Thugamar suas dár n-aistear.
Níorbh fhéidir dul don Chaladh.
Chasamar *An Maoilín*
is thugamar faoi'n mbaile.

Le sá na maidí rámha
léim Maoilín chun rásaíochta.
Ach bhí Pangar Dubh inár ndiaidh
le scríob, le tonn ár smísteadh.

Chuir sé an mhuir ag luascadh
le béimeanna dá eireaball.
Chaith sé seilí leis an spéir
gur dalladh muid le fearthainn.

Ach ghlaoigh an Sceilg orainn
le teanga iarainn tomhaiste
a leath paróiste Dé
chugainn amach thar bhócna.

Bráithre ar an Ard
ár ngríosadh is ár ngairmeadh
'Seachain Splinc na mBroigheall.
Gabh amach níos faide!
Níos faide fós! Níos faide!'

Thugamar an Maoilín
thart faoin Splinc ar éigin,
ár maidí rámha ag giascán,
muid féin i ndeireadh déithe.

Leis an réim a bhí faoi Phangar,
sháraíomar é sa chasadh.
Shroiseamar Cuas na Nae.
'Chríost nár dhiamhair í an tarrach!

An tonn mar tharbh ag láth
Maoilín chomh cas le gamhain
is mura mbeadh ag Dia
bháifí muid sa chaladh.

Lámha láidre, greim,
tuairteáil agus tarraingt
súgán agus rón
leathbhá, liúr, gearradh.

Maoilín slán ar chéibhe.
Muid uilig tugtha tnáite
ach an cat ag ródaíocht fós
á chruinniú féin don áladh.

Le rópaí daingne láidre
cheanglaíomar ár mbáidín
B'í a bhí ina moirt
ina leidhbín leamh, báite.

Ach le cabhair ó Dhia na Glóire
is taca óna mháithrín
is le heifeacht na n-ullóg
thugamar í in airde.

An cat á únfairt féin
thíos ag bun na faille,
an Sceilg, aonlong Dé
beag beann ar fhiúr na mara.

Seán Lysaght

Gannets

Rich neighbours
Sailing their big yachts
All over the sound.
The stadium packed full
Of their supporters.
Look at those blue nests
Built with someone's ropes.
That's thrifty!

Follow one with your envy,
Watch him fold his wings
To deliver a killer blow
To a life several feet below the surface.
He makes it look easy.

Close-up, this goose
Is armed with a dagger,
Takes off from the water
In a clatter of splash,
And goes home.

You stand your ground a mile away,
Watch them at the gannetry,
Lazy white motes floating
Like the flakes in a snow globe
Settling slowly.

Storm Petrels

Pilgrims at midnight,
Our flashlamps climbing the stairs,
We had a scuffle with buffetings
On the last flight
And crept up on all fours
Under the lid of the wind.

The enclosure steadied us.
Wall and corbelling
Had been heaped for so long
Chink by chink, we could not go wrong,
And the hutch of stone was heaviest
At the very top, to make us strong.

Darkness was a swarm
Of darker fragments, of wills
Briefly flickering in my beam.
These were said to be the souls
Of dead monks coming home
On a gust to their star garden.

There was one, atop a wall,
Trapped in the dazzle of our light!
He had dancing shoes for the sea,
Little black webbed feet,
And each beaded eye of Biscay
Shone with its original star.

To conquer this dark
Another age painted terror—
But none was here.
I fingered the plumage gently
And blessed our reverent heads
With a motto: *Never fear.*
The boats are coming back.
This will be remembered
In a gurgle and a small click you hear
When you listen at the stone gap.'

Eiléan Ní Chuilleanáin

Vertigo

1. The Litany

As every new day waking finds its pitch
Selecting a fresh angle, so the sun
Hangs down its veils, so the ancient verbs
Change their invocation and their mood.

Steady through the long gap in the story
A stiff breeze whistles up off the ocean
Choosing a pair of notes, the same key.

A tidal drag sucks back down as deep
As it rode high; the foamy-crested wave
(Astonished at numbers, the white gannets,
In their salt generations) arrives
To listen for that high voice and stays,
Arching smoothly, waiting for the response.

The soaking tears of centuries drill down
Low passages in between the stones,
Holding to the calendar made out

In columns of names, a single stiff skin
Coiled up and stowed away in the high slit
Above the stone corbel that once had human features.

The wave can pause no longer, called back to Brazil.

2. The Storm

What am I doing here, says the old strong voice,
The wave reaching and snatching
Around the pinnacles, faltering and returning
To fling its quilt across the sloping stone
Where in the softer days the seal took a rest;
So it wells up, squirting up roses in its fall,
Trying again, the awful repeated recoil,
And where is truth under the slamming and roaring,
It wants to know, and *where*,
Where is pity now? Gone below,
Wiped from the view, and indeed
What has happened to time, as the day's news
Is repeated, bellowing like the storm?

3. Indoors

Look in the iced-up glass:
Can you read the shadowy blotches,
Are those fish, skeletal boats
Learning low tide?

The alabaster lamp reflects
Almost the whole dark day, measuring
Light on the veined stone fireplace,
Its curdled white and grey

The map of a language
Spilling across a border
Words retreating back in the throat,
The tight mountainous enclave,

As in the five days she lay without a word,
Five glasses of milk huddled on a shelf,
Congealed, the sun of a winter afternoon
Breaking through curtains, piercing the shining whey.

4. Direction

Searching about again to find my father
I must take a step backwards, for in the time
Since last I saw him he has moved and changed
More than in all of his life:

He is a mountain becoming a mountain range,
A sliding dance of peaks, their names picked from his list,
The words remembered from the internment camp,
That gave him his phobia of candles, his cardplaying codes,
The pipe he never smoked with its ivory bowl.

As he believed that foreign words were real,
Their declension revealing even what crawled away
Refusing to be learned—in that belief

So many anxieties he shed, he leaves
Me what I would leave behind for you:

They need not last forever;
They need not lay you forever low.

5. Outdoors

In summer the rain falls slowly at the junction,
The bushes have grown, hiding the station sign.
The holly tree we knew so well is taller
So the clock on the town hall tower no longer tells us the time—

Nobody thinks we'll go on our travels again:
Hunger and cold and carrying loads are all
Far away, the wind and the birds' famished complaint,
Far as the moving tanker on the grey horizon, as hardly gained;
Until the morning when the mist rises at six,
The shadows sit up, a thrush on a branch speaks his mind,
Somewhere a boat swings away from the stone steps,
An engine kicks and stammers again until it fires.

6. Vertigo

Shaped like a barrel with asthma, her black skirt
Bunched at her waist, she kneels or squats
At every spot reputed to be holy.
Her two daughters wait and gossip until
She scrambles up and they move a few yards on.

How did such smart women acquire such a mother?
She insists on doing the next bit barefoot. 'Nobody
Does that any more, Mama.' But she's down,
One haunch on a pointed stone, handing the shoes
To the younger one, hauling off the black stockings

Which she adds to the black bag, already encumbered
With rosary beads tangled in keys, all the stuff
She's dragged from home. She struggles ahead,
Joining the queue to climb the staggered steps
Along the cliff edge. A puffin lands beside her;

She yelps in surprise. Then she reaches out in her turn
To stroke each of five crosses cut in the slab,
Then off again. The daughters are resigned
To the last sharp ascent. From below, they keep her
In sight. The mainland spreads in the wide distance;

The clouds are scattering, and above them stands
The abbey's stony north face, and the great door—
But photography barely exists. The lighthouse-men
Have news of the Russian war. The daughters fret,
Watching the bumblebees trample the sea-pinks

In the spot where last year a man fell and smashed,
How will they ever get her back down to the boat?
She is terrified of heights. The seagulls' diving call,
The foam at the foot of the cliff, make her feel sick,
But she does look down, and at last sees what is there,

The dimensions, the naming. Yes.
A broad slick widening, an anachronism,
Ambiguous like a leaf floating where never
A leaf has blown, like a word, a calque, swimming
Up into sight through the tides of speech, like a seal
Playing on the deep ocean:
                                   the gate of her days left open,
Her daughters like armed angels guarding each side
Of the path to the edge, where everything pours away.

Nuala Ní Dhomhnaill

Díseart na Sceilge

Súim ar lantán aerach
atá gearrtha amach ag na manaigh
snoite síos go dtí an bhunshraith,
féith gheal den gcloch scáil.

Tá faobhar na gcloch 'am ghearradh.
Bhéadh sé níos measa dá mbeinn ar mo ghlúine,
ag móradh Rí na nDúl
is an phian ag dul isteach go dtí an chnámh.

Níl rud ar bith le feiscint
ach suathadh an Aitleantaigh
is i bhfad ar chlé tá scáthshlios
de fhailltreacha Uibh Ráthaigh.

Tá loinnir ar an uisce
a chuirfeadh tú ar meisce.
Níl aon ní os mo chionn in airde,
nil éinne (dá mbeadh sé ann) ach Dia amháin.

Tá folús glan im' aigne
nach dtuigeann beo nó marbh,
nach mbraitheann ach an noiméad
síoraí seo ina iomláine.

Cé thóg an struchtúr cloiche,
an falla seo ar crochadh
os cionn an duibheagáin
is neamhní uafar an spáis?

Skellig Hermitage

I sit on an airy terrace
hewn out by the monks,
peeled down to the substratum,
a bright vein of reflective rock.

The bladed rock cuts into me.
It would be worse if I were kneeling,
praising the King of the Elements
while pain cut to the bone.

There is nothing to be seen
but the swelling of the Atlantic
and far leftward the shadowed layers
of the Iveragh cliffs.

The water gleams
intoxicatingly.
There is nothing over my head,
nobody but (if he were there) God.

An emptiness in my mind
comprehends neither quick nor dead,
absorbs only this moment,
eternal, whole.

Who built the stone structure,
this wall suspended
over the abyss
and the awful nothing of space?

An rabhadar uile ar mire
le grá Dé is fuath don duine
imithe le haer an tsaoil
nach é an saol seo é amháin?

Ar cruthaíodh mícró-aeráid
i gcoinne scallaí árda gaoithe
is stoirmeacha ró-dhiamhara
an Aitleantaigh Thuaidh?

Nó ar tugadh dúshlán na síne
na gcamfheothan is na díle
mar chros an mhairtírigh creidimh
ar son na fulaingthe ann féin?

Is cuma liom ar deireadh.
Níl ann ach mé féin is an neamhní,
an bríos gaoithe is an ghrian
ag drithliú ar an aigéan.

Seinntear anseo ceol síoraí
na néanlaithe is na gaoithe.
I bhfad thíos tá sceamhaíl na rónta
as na tonntracha ag briseadh ar an bhfaill.

Níl rud ar bith anseo ach an fharraige mhór
ag síneadh go híor na spéire os mo chomhair.

Were all their wits astray
in loving God and hating their own,
gone with the wind of a world
not this world only?

Was a microclimate created
against high squalls of wind
and the omnipotent storms
of the North Atlantic?

Or was defiance flung at rough weather,
at foul wind and at flood
as a cross for faith's martyrdom,
for the very sake of suffering?

To me, after all, it's all the one.
There is just myself and nothingness,
the wind, and the sun
glittering on the ocean.

Here is played the unending music
of birds, and of the wind.
Far below, seals wail
from waves breaking on a cliff.

Here there is nothing but the wide, wide sea
stretching to horizons beyond my reach.

Éanlaith na Sceilge

(i)

Do scríobhas i ndán fadó fadó
go raibh naomh ar an Sceilg
is fuiseoga ag eitilt timpeall air.
Anois nó go rabhas amuigh ar an gcarraig
tuigim go raibh sé sin dodhéanta,
fiú dá mba naomh féin é. Bíonn móinéar
ón bhfuiseog chun a nead a dhéanamh
is níl oiread talamh leibhéalta amuigh ar an gcreig
is a chuirfeadh manach. Ní fhágann san, áfach,
nach bhfuil an cloch ar fad ag preabadh beo
le héanlaith.

(ii)

Ní rabhamar tagtha in aon ghaobhar in aon chor
don gcarraig nuair a chonac mo chéad éan dearg.
Do dh'eitil sé go híseal taobh linn.
Bhí cuma chomh haisteach sin ar an éan
—aghaidh fidil air ar nós fir seoigh—
gur bhuaileas mo bhosa ar a chéile
go sceitimíneach ar nós níonáin. 'Fuipín'
arsa mise agus mé ins na trithí gáirí.
'Fuipín, fuipín, fuipín , fuipín'.
Thug lucht an bháid neamháird
ar mo chuid geaitsí.
'Chífidh tú go leor eile díobh san fós'
ar siad. Rud ab fhíor go maith dóibh.

Birds of Skellig

(i)

In a long ago poem I wrote
that there was a monk on Skellig
with larks in flight around him.
Now that I've been out on the rock
I understand that this was not possible,
even for a saint. A meadow
is what a lark needs to nest in
and there isn't as much land on the crag
as would bury a monk. That, however, is not
to say the rock is not every inch of it
alive with birds.

(ii)

We hadn't really come alongside
the rock when I saw my first red bird.
He flew in low and close beside us.
He looked so absolutely ludicrous
—a mask on him like a circus clown—
that I clapped my hands together
as giddily as a child. 'Puffin'
says I in a fit of the giggles,
'Fuipín, fuipín, fuipín, fuipín'.
The crowd in the boat acted like
I was for the birds.
'You'll see plenty of them yet,'
they said. And they were dead right.

(iii)

Bhí forachain agus crosáin
ina gcéadtaibh agus ina gcomhthaláin
amuigh ar bhinsí os cionn an ché istigh.

Chuimhníos ar an méid adúirt Maidhc Pheig Sayers
i dtaobh mhuintir an Oileáin
nuair a thagadh lá breá san Aibreán
go mbídís seo ar gor
ina Inis na Bró agus sa Tiaracht.

D'imíodh na hOileánaigh siar
le naomhóga agus slait fada acu
agus súil ribe i mbarr gach slaite.

Bhíodh na forachain agus na crosáin
is a gceann amach thar faobhar gach binse acu
leis an ngréin. Thagadh an naomhóg faoina mbun
is ní bhíodh ach an slat a shíneadh in airde
is an súil ribe a chur ar mhuineál an éin
is é a tharrach chugat. Ní mó ná
go bhfanfaidís go mbéarfá led' láimh orthu.

Nuair a bhíodh beirt ón dtigh in aon naomhóg amháin
b'fhéidir go mbeadh deich dosaen acu ag teacht tráthnóna.
San am is go mbídís sin priocaithe, giobaithe, nite, glan
ag bean an tí, ní mór an teaspach a bheadh uirthi.
Ansan chuirtí ar salann iad.
D'ithtí úr leis iad, iad a róstadh ar an dtlú
nó iad a bheiriú. Ba mhaith beirithe i sciléad iad.

Choimeádaidís an clúmh le cur i dtochtanna.

(iii)

There were guillemots and razorbills
arrayed in ranks and files
out on ledges above the pier.

I remembered what Maidhc Pheig Sayers said
about the Blasket people
on a fine April day
when these were hatching
in Inis na Bró and Tiaracht.

The islanders would go out
in canoes, carrying long rods
with a looped snare at the tip of each rod.

The guillemots and razorbills
had their heads out over the edge of each ledge,
taking the sun. The canoe came underneath
and you needed only to stretch the rod up
and loop the snare around the bird's neck
and jerk it to you. They just about
waited for you to grab them.

If there were two from any house in the one canoe
they might have ten dozen coming home that evening.
By the time they were picked, plucked, washed and cleaned
by bean a' tí, she was a quiet woman.
Then they were salted.
They were eaten fresh too, roasted on the tongs
or boiled. They were good boiled in a skillet.

The plumage was kept to be put in quilts.

(iv)

Tá fuipíní anois ar an Sceilg go hanaman na marbh
is níl éinne á bhfiach nó á seilg.
Ach fadó, Muintir an Oileáin Tiar
bhainidís cuid caite astu go fíor.

(v)

An Méid Adúirt Maidhc Pheig Sayers dtaobh na gCánóg nDubh

Éan dubh is ea í seo agu brollach bán aici
agus í bán i dtaobh istigh do na sciatháin.
Tá gob cam tanaí uirthi. Bíonn boladh láidir uaithi
mar is ar íle a bhíonn ar an bhfarraige a mhaireann sí.
Istigh faoi chloch nó i bpoll coinín go mbeadh daingniú
cloiche air a dheineann sí a nead.
Le seans a bhéarfá ar chánóg óg.
Fothaíoch a thugann siad air sin.

Chloisfeá istoíche an chánóg ag gabháil thar tigh
agus feadaíl aici. Bíonn an fothaíoch i bhfad Éireann
don bhliain a thógaint ag an gcánóig agus bíonn sé reamhar
agus is ar éigean a chífeá aon tsúil ann.
Bíonn siad an-dheas le n-ithe ach ní bhíodh éacht acu le fáil.

(vi)

Chuala-sa, leis, an chánóg dhubh ag feadaíl san oíche
is mé amuigh ar an Sceilg. Chuala chomh maith na guardail
is iad ag ag meamhlach ar nós cait stigh sa 'drywall'.
Ba dhóigh leat gur ina bheatha a bhí an cloch ar fad leo mar éanlaith.

Sin a bhfuil de scéala agam ar éanlaith na Sceilge.

(iv)

There are puffins now on Skellig forever and a day
and nobody hunts high up or low down for them.
But long ago, the people of the Western Island
made use of them to the very last.

(v)

What Maidhc Pheig Sayers said about the Shearwater

This is a black bird with a white breast
with white on the underside of the wings.
She has a narrow, curved beak. She has a strong smell
because she lives on the oil of the sea.
Under a stone or in a rabbit's burrow strengthened
by stone is where she nests.
You'd be lucky to catch a young shearwater.
A *fothaíoch* is what it's called.

By night you'd hear the shearwater passing the house,
whistling. The *fothaíoch* spends a great part of the year
being reared by the shearwater and he gets fat
and you would barely see his eyes.
They are good to eat, but you'd never get many of them.

(vi)

I too heard the shearwater whistling by night
when I was out on Skellig. I heard also the storm petrels
mewing like cats in the drystone wall.
You would think the rock was alive with them.

And that is all I have to say about the Skellig birds.

Annálacha Díseart na Sceilge

A.D. 805 Labhair aingeal le duine des na manaigh ar an Sceilg agus dúirt leis dul in airde go barra na cloiche ó dheas agus aireagal a thógaint ann. Do chabhraigh na manaigh eile leis. Ba phaidir í gach cloch. *Laborare est orare.* Do ghearradar amach céimeanna trí Chró na Snáthaide is thógadar na fallaí ann. Do shnoíodar báisíní chun uisce báistí a bhailiú iontu. Tógadh lantán beag mar gharraí. Bhí cion fir de shlí ann.

A.D. 815 Shéid an ghaoth i scallaí arda. Bhi caortha dearga fearthain is tóirneach ann. Bhí an spéir ar lasadh is an fharraige glégheal. Do thit turlabhait báistí anuas ar an díthreabhach. Bhí sé ag creathadh le fuacht agus é báite go craiceann. Bhí camfheothan chomh fiáin ag bualadh na cloiche gur dheacair dó a cheann a ardú. Ní raibh aon trua age dó féin mar *seo é ár ndiúltiú dúinn féin, nach scaoilimíd dár mianta is go séanaimíd ár bpeacaí. Is é seo ár dtógáil na croise orainn féin agus ár nglacadh le cailliúint agus mairtíreacht agus fulaingt ar son Chríosta.*

A.D.824 Do chreach na Lochlannaigh Mainistir na Sceilge ach níor taibhríodh riamh dóibh go mbeadh díseart ar barr na binne ó dheas. D'fhan an díthreabhach i bhfolach gur imíodar is ansan thug buíochas do Dhia. Ní raibh éinne eile fágtha ar an Sceilg. Thugadar leo Etgal, an t-ab, is fuair sé bás ina dhiaidh sin ina measc de ghorta.

A.D 836 Bhí an díthreabhach ina fhear faire ag barr na binne theas. Chonaic sé an cabhlach Lochlannach ag teacht. Theich na manaigh ón mainistir suas trí Chró na Snáthaide go dtí an t-aireagal. Nuair a shrois na Lochlannaigh an mhainistir ní raibh Críostaí Mhic an Luain rómpú. D'éirigh siad as an bhfuadach ansan.

The Annals of the Skellig Hermitage

A.D. 806   An angel spoke to one of the monks on Skellig and told him to climb the peak to the south and build an oratory there. The other monks helped him. Each stone was a prayer. *Laborare est orare.* They carved steps through the Eye of the Needle and built walls. They sculpted basins to gather rainwater. They built a small terrace for a garden. There was space enough for one man.

A.D. 815   There were great blasts of wind. There were red fireballs, there was rain and thunder. The sky was alight and the sea glowed. A great downrush of rain fell on the hermit. He was shaking with cold and soaked to the skin. A foul wind was beating the rock so wildly that he could barely raise his head. He took no pity on himself because *this is our denial of our self, that we do not indulge our desires and that we reject sin. This is our shouldering of the cross and our acceptance of loss and of martyrdom and of suffering for Christ.*

A.D. 824   The Vikings plundered Skellig monastery but never imagined that there could be a hermitage on the South Peak. The hermit waited in hiding until they had gone and then gave thanks to God. There was nobody else left on Skellig. They had taken Etgal, the abbot, who afterwards died among them, from hunger.

A.D. 836   The hermit was on watch at the summit of the South Peak. He saw the Viking fleet approaching. The monks fled the monastery up through the Eye of the Needle to the oratory. When the Vikings reached the monastery, not a trace of a Christian soul was before them. They abandoned the search.

A.D 847   An turas seo bhí an díthreabhach ina chodladh ar chuma Chon Crithir ag Cath Fionn Trá. Tháinig loingeas ó Luimneach i ndeisceart na hÉireann agus chreachadar Sceilg agus Inis Fáil agus Dísirt Donnain agus Cluain Mór agus mharaíodar Rudgaile MacTrebhthaidh, agus Cormac Mac Selbhaig, an díthreabhach. Is é siúd an té gur scaoil an t-aingeal na ceangail air dhá huaire is gur cheangail na Gaill faoi dhó arís é gach uair.

A.D.920   Shiúl an díthreabhach deireanach timpeall ar an lantán caol ós comhair an aireagail, ag canadh sailm naofa, leath as Gaeilge, leath as Laidin:
> Deus meus adiuva me.
> Tabhair dom do chabhair a Aon-Mhic Dé.
> Tabhair dom do chabhair, a Aon-Mhic Dé.
> Deus meus adiuva me.

A.D. 950   Fuair Bláthmhac na Sceilge bás.

A.D. 995   Chonaic manaigh na mainistreach cath ollmhór sa spéir, ina raibh na deamhain ag troid in aghaidh fórsaí Dé, faoi cheannas Mhichíl Naofa, Ard-aingeal. Do bhuaigh an naomh ar na deamhain agus ina dhiaidh sin tionlacaíodh an charraig do Naomh Mícheál agus dhein Sceilg Mhichíl de.

A.D. 1044   I mbliain seo ár dTiarna, Aodh Sceilg Mhichíl, an sagart oirearc, aontumhach agus an té ba naofa ar fad ar na Gael uile, do luigh sé siar i mbachlainn Chríost.

A.D. 1230   D'imigh an aimsir in olcas bliain i ndiaidh bliana. Cheap na manaigh gur chucu an Díleann. Sa bhliain seo conacthas sliabh mór leac oighir amuigh sa bhfarraige. Dhearbhaigh na manaigh go raibh sé in am Mainistir na Sceilge a thréigint agus dul chun cónaithe sa mhainistir i mBaile an Sceilg. Théidís amach ann i rith an tsamhraidh, san aimsir bhreá i dteannta na n-oilithreach.

A.D. 847   On this occasion the hermit was in a sleep as deep as that of Conn Crithear at the Battle of Ventry. A fleet came from Limerick in the south of Ireland and they plundered Skellig and Inis Fáil and Díseart Donnain and Cluain Mór and they killed Rudgaile Mac Trebthaidh, and Cormac Mac Selbhaigh, the hermit. He is the one whose bonds the angel twice released and whom each time the Vikings tied up again.

A.D. 920   The last hermit walked around the narrow terrace in front of the oratory, singing a sacred psalm, alternating between Irish and Latin:
>   Deus meus adiuva me.
>   Tabhair dom do chabhair, a Aon-Mhic Dé.
>   Tabhair dom do chabhair, a Aon-Mhic Dé.
>   Deus meus adiuva me.

A.D. 950   Bláthmhac of Skellig died.

A.D. 995   The monks of the monastery saw an enormous battle in the sky, in which the devils fought against the forces of God under the command of Saint Michael the Archangel. The saint defeated the devils and afterwards the rock was dedicated to Saint Michael and became Skellig Michael.

A.D. 1044   In this year of the Lord, Aodh of Skellig Michael, the eminent cleric, celibate and the holiest of all among the Gaels, reposed in the embrace of Christ.

A.D. 1230   The weather became worse year after year. The monks thought that the Apocalypse was approaching. In this year a great mountain of ice was seen out to sea. The monks affirmed that it was time to abandon the monastery of Skellig and to take up residence in the monastery in Ballinskelligs. They would go back out in summer, in clement weather, along with the pilgrims.

A.D. 1725   Ghaibh mórán oilithreach an cosáinín anacrach trí Chró na Snáthaide go barr na binne ó dheas. Do ghaibheadar go mall is go cúramach ar scaradh gabhail órlach i ndiaidh orlaigh go dtí gur phógadar an leac a bhí ina sheasamh amuigh ar bharr na binne. Ghearr duine éigin croíláidir acu cros beag ar an leac.

A.D. 1825   Fós bhí mórán oilithreach ag déanamh a slí suas an cosáinín, ag tabhairt turais na Sceilge. Ní chomhairítí an turas mura bpógaidís an leac a bhí amuigh ar an mBior, is go ndeiridís an 'Ár nAthair' amuigh ann. Thugaidís Nead an Iolair ar an ionad seo toisc é bheith thuas san aer. Ní dócha gur thóg siad aon cheann nó go dtug siad faoi ndeara na scamaill ag snámh go sochmhar ós a gcionn, nó suathadh na mara móire faoina mbonn. Ní dócha gurb é áilleacht an radhairc is mó a bhí ag dó na geirbe orthu ach sábháilteacht a gcraiceann féin.

A.D. 1851   Tháinig an t-ársaitheoir Windele go dtí an Sceilg, is bhí sceon agus uamhan air ag siúl suas na céimeanna go dti an Diallait. Ní raibh seans faoin spéir go dtabharfadh sé faoi chosán na n-oilithreach, suas tré Chró na Snáthaide go dtí barr na binne ó dheas. D'fhéach sé ar an meall mór cloiche 'a éiríonn aníos ón nDiallait go hairde abhálmhór atá geall le bheith ingearach'.

A.D. 1869   Dhreap Edwin Richard Wyndham-Quin, an tríú iarla Dunraven, go barr na binne theas. Ba é an chéad ársaitheoir a dhein é. Strapaire óg ab ea é agus níorbh aon nath dó deacracht na slí. Is é an chéad ársaitheoir a thug faoi ndeara an díseart. Ar seisean ina leabhar a foilsíodh i 1875 ' In aice na háite is airde ar a dtugann siad an Bior thángas ar iarsmaí foirgnimh bhig a raibh cuma dronnuilleogach air, agus gur dócha gur aireagal a bhí ann. Tá ursain amháin de dhoras le feiscint agus crosleac cóngarach dó. Tá gach cosúlacht ann gurb é seo an áit atá marcáilte mar "ionad adhlactha" i léarscáil an tSuirbhé Ordanáis.'

A.D. 1725   Many pilgrims took the penitential path through the Eye of the Needle to the top of the South Peak. They went slowly and carefully, astride the ledge inch upon inch until they kissed the slab out at the summit. Some brave heart among them carved a small cross on the slab.

A.D. 1825   There were still many pilgrims making their way up the small path, making the Skellig visitation. It did not count as a visitation if they did not kiss the slab out at the Point, and say the 'Our Father' out there. They named this place the Eagle's Nest because of its loftiness. They probably never paid attention to, or even noticed, the clouds floating placidly above or the swelling of the great ocean below. The spectacular view was probably of far less concern to them than was saving their own skins.

A.D. 1851   The antiquarian Windele went to Skellig, and was filled with fear and dread walking up the steps to the Saddle. There was no chance whatsoever that he would take the pilgrims' path up through the Eye of the Needle to the top of the South Peak. He looked at the great mass of stone 'which arose at one side of it at an immense height nearly perpendicularly'.

A.D. 1869   Edwin Richard Wyndham-Quin, the third Earl of Dunraven, climbed the South Peak. He was the first antiquarian to do so. He was a strapping young man, and the climb presented little difficulty. He was the first antiquarian to notice the hermitage. In his book published in 1875 he wrote: 'Near the highest point of the island, which is called the Spit, I found the remains of a little building which appears to have been quadrangular, probably an oratory—all that now remains are portions of the south and west walls, with one jamb of the doorway and a cross standing near. This is probably the spot which is marked 'burying place' in the map of the Ordnance Survey. There are also curious portions of an ancient wall on certain projections of rock near the Spit.'

A.D. 1952   Dhein Liam de Paor staidéar ar an Sceilg ach níor dhreap sé suas an Bhinn Theas. Thug sé faoi ndeara, áfach go raibh struchtúir tógtha air ag láimh an duine.

A.D. 1957   Tá ráiteas níos foirleithne ag Francoise Henri ar dhíseart na Sceilge ná mar atá ag éinne a chuaigh roimpi. Níor dhreap sí féin suas ann áfach, ach chuaigh duine de fhir coimeádta an tsolais ann di. Mr. Eugene Gillan ab ainm dó . Tharraing sé pictiúr beag de lantán an aireagail di, a chuir sí i gcló.

A.D. 1977   Thit an leac ar barr na binne le linn mór-stoirme. Cuardaíodh ar an nDiallait é agus fiú chuaigh tomadóirí á lorg sa bhfarraige ach ní bhfuarthas ó shoin aon rian dó.

A.D. 1981   Chuaigh dream seandálaithe suas ar an mBinn Theas agus d'aithníodar gur Díseart a bhí ann, tógtha mar a bheadh sé san aer. Ní go dtí go raibh sé dreaptha acu cúpla huair a dheineadar amach cad a bhí ann, leis an alltacht a chuir an áit orthu. De réir a chéile ghlanadar an cairpéid den gcoireán mara a bhí ag fás ann agus nochtadh lantáin na manach.

A.D. 1990   Scríobhadar leabhar ag foilsiú don domhain an t-iontas is an fhionnachtain dochreidte a taibhsíodh dóibh.

A.D. 2008   Le rópaí ceangailte dem chabhail is le caoin-chabhair ós na heolaithe, do dhreap an t-oilithreach bocht seo suas an Binn. Ba pheata lae é, is bhí solas gléineach ar an aigéan. Ba dhóigh leat gur sciath airgid é ag frithchaitheamh solas na gréine. D'imigh an t-uamhan agus an t-eagla díom, an t-anbhá is an sceimhle. Cé go raibh gach coiscéim suas mar choiscéim i dtreo mo bháis agam thángas anuas ar nos cait. Bhíos mar bháirneach ar an gcloich. Thuigeas na díseartaigh, a ngáirdeas is a mbioth. Thuigeas a n-uabhar chomh maith.

A.D. 1952   Liam de Paor investigated Skellig, but did not climb the South Peak. He did note, however, that a structure had been built on it.

A.D. 1957   Françoise Hardy published a more comprehensive account of the Skellig hermitage than any previous one. She did not climb there herself, but a lighthouse keeper did so for her. He was a Mr. Eugene Gillan. He drew a small picture of the oratory terrace, which she published.

A.D. 1977   The slab at the peak's summit fell during a great storm. It was searched for on the Saddle and divers even searched the seabed for it, but no trace of it has ever been discovered.

A.D. 1981   A small group of archaeologists climbed the South Peak and recognised that it was a hermitage, built, as it were, on air. It was not until they had climbed it a few awestruck times that they discerned what was there. Gradually they cleared the carpet of the sea campion that grew there and the monks' terraces were revealed.

A.D. 1990   They wrote a book announcing to the world the wonder and the incredible discovery that had appeared to them.

A.D. 2008   With ropes attached, and calmed by the support of the initiates, this poor pilgrim climbed the South Peak. It was a pet day, and light gleamed on the ocean, a silver shield reflecting the sunlight. Horror and fear fell away from me, panic and terror left me. Although each step I climbed up was like a step to my own death, I came down like a cat. I could cling to the rock like a limpet. I understood the hermits, their celebratory universe. Their pride, too, I understood.

Bernard O'Donoghue

Out in the Weather

> There I took my pleasure in the gannet's cry
> and curlew's melody instead of men's laughter,
> in the sea-gull's song rather than mead-drinking.
> —*The Seafarer*

There are many great monastic poems in Old Irish: fewer in English. But probably the greatest monastic poem in English is the Anglo-Saxon poem called 'The Seafarer' which is an exhilarating evocation of the sea and storms and the birds that live at sea. There is a famous puzzle about it though: after describing with great force the intolerable pain and hardship of life on the sea, the poem suddenly says 'And therefore the heart's thoughts now urge me that I should explore for myself the high floods, the sea's salt-waves'. Why 'therefore', if the pains of seafaring are so terrible? In order to explain this paradox, scholars of Old English poetry have invoked a famous story told in the Anglo-Saxon Chronicle. In the time of King Alfred in the late 9th century, two monks were washed up on the shore of the south of England, in a small boat without oars. They explained that they were Irish monks who had cast themselves off to sea in this precarious way as part of a *peregrinatio pro amore Dei:* 'as a pilgrimage for the love of God'. I had always thought of this as a likeable kind of religious myth. But after getting to know in June 2009 something about monastic life on the Skellig, it seems much more than that. Let me explain.

To start with, we drove west from Cork airport in what proved to be the last spell of real summer weather for the year on 26th June, through Baile Mhuirne and Killarney, and then on along the spectacular Ballaghasheen road (Bealach Oisín, of course), only stopping at the Climbers Inn at Glencar for a drink in memory of Herbert MacCabe's summer schools in the 1980s. In the evening in Waterville we all walked along the beautiful stony shore before sitting in the house of Fíona and Paddy Bushe which is a sanctuary of writing and art and music, watching the sun setting over Bá na Scealg.

Next morning we are on the quayside at Portmagee where we meet Des Lavelle. I tell him I have been reading his *Skellig Story* in the Bodleian Library two days before: he is gracious and friendly but impressively unimpressed by my information. It is obvious to anyone that this harbour is a better place to be than the Bodleian. Then we all set off in Eoin Walsh's orange boat, past the small monastic island of Illaunloughan in Portmagee harbour (I don't yet grasp the significance of that either), and I find myself half-remembering the great Irish poems that begin with this kind of embarkation: "on the deck of Patrick Lynch's boat", and the rest. It evokes English poems too, of course, especially 'Flannan Isle' as the "day broke blue and bright, / With glancing sun and glancing spray, / As o'er the swell our boat made way, / As gallant as a gull in flight." Have I ever done anything more wonderful and invigorating? Eoin tells us that, despite the spectacular weather now—hot sun and skin cream—there will be no boats tomorrow because there will be a Force Seven gale blowing. Can this be true?

The first extraordinary thing in this day full of extraordinary things is that Eoin takes us right in under the lee of the Little Skellig with its 20,000 gannets above us. We had started to see the odd gannet from the shore—"like a blown outrider from a beehive", I have called it in a poem; but their density here is hard to believe as you watch it. Yet no matter how many of them there are, one by one they never fail to make your heart beat faster, more than any other bird.

> Gulls can't contain their loud excitement,
> shrilling, bickering away at anything.
> The oyster-catchers are as bad, punctuating
> their anxious cries with sprints along the shore
> or suddenly flocking to find a better pasture.
> But the gannet's above all that. He wings alone
> and silent, jet-powered in an age of turbo-props.
> Like the single bee, a blown outrider
> from the crowded hive, he takes his time to it,
> winging his own way home to the Skelligs.

Paddy points out to us the channel by which another boatman used to steer through the base of the island. We are accompanied on the boat by a group of excited Japanese women of my kind of age; they are charmed and giggly when Eoin ('a handsome boatman', to quote 'Carrickfergus') asks them for their passports as we draw in to the island. Paddy tells me he was on the boat during the drawn Cork-Kerry Munster football semi-final and Eoin's steering became precarious as the match approached its nailbiting climax. Also on the boat is a black-and-white sheepdog which stands by the rail, tongue lolling and beaming at the sea, like our farm dogs in the car in the 1950s.

We are met at the East landing stage at Blind Man's Cove by Catherine, the glamorous Board of Works warden. I remember her from the cafe on the Great Blasket: she knows how to pick her placements! We trudge in the hot sun up the path by the South Landing, to the four Board of Works huts where we are to spend the next three days: extraordinary bliss! My hut belongs to the health officer of the OPW, Paddy thinks, and it is full of untouchable items of high quality: pink grapefruit, a five-stringed guitar, hazelnuts and peaches. My window looks across the Atlantic towards Ballinskelligs, so I am exactly opposite Bolus Head, but now to the north of it. Last year I was due south of the same point in Eyeries, looking at the other side of it from my northfacing room in the writers' retreat Anam Cara. How many such spectacular points are there in this south-western corner of Ireland? So we are now at the spot where Kenneth Clark says European civilisation began. There is a puffin on my window-sill, looking hot and bothered. We will see thousands of them—in different weathers—over the coming days.

The last boats leave for the mainland at 3.00, taking back our Japanese friends and everyone else. So now it is us on Sceilg Mhichíl, and the rest of humanity back where they belong in the world. We alone are living out in the weather, experiencing as Bernard Shaw said a "magic that takes you out, far out, of this time and this world". We start by climbing up to the monastery under the hot sun. We can hear the puffin-calls which, as Paddy says, sound exactly like an electric hedge-trimmer being revved up a couple of fields away. Which analogy came first, the puffin or the trimmer? It's like the internal combustion engine and its resemblance to the highly-tuned cardiac blood-pumping system. The 600-step path to the monastery seems less long than I remember, but much more precipitous. At the last corner, above Christ's Saddle, there is a windy corner before the last flight of steps, leading into the monks' garden. When we came here with Fr. Matt Keane in 1993, I came back down from the top to urge him (he was 76) up to the end: one of the few interventions in someone else's life I am proud of. Now I find it hard to make myself go.

This is nothing, of course: we will learn that to get a full sense of words like 'vertiginous' and 'precarious' and their etymologies, you have to approach the hermitage on the South Peak, to the west of the island. To get a sense of that from the page, you must find the wonderful book that was on the table in my hut: *The Forgotten Hermitage of Skellig Michael* by Walter Horn, Jenny White Marshall and Grellan D. Rourke. [1990 University of California Press: reprinted sumptuously by the Irish DOE Dúchas 2002] It is the most hauntingly beautiful book, and it would certainly be my desert island book. I suppose it already is a 'Desert Island' book, since this monastic island is devoted to the observances of the Egyptian Desert followers of St. Anthony, after which are named the various Irish 'Dyserts'. To get a full sense of 'vertiginous', look at the picture on page 59 of a young woman lifting a carefree, bejeaned leg over the sea with the Little Skellig beyond her.

But back to our more cautious climb. The wind is getting up, hot as the sun is: maybe Eoin's Force 7 is on the way. Many things have been improved by the Board of Works since 1993, giving a much better sense of what the monastery was like and how it operated, especially the long periphery wall below the beehive huts. I repeat the photograph everyone takes, of the snail-shaped window framing the Little Skellig against the blue sea: I suppose my favourite view in the world. "You and 10,000 others," Paddy says rightly. Flat on the ground here is a sad grave inscription, to 'Patrick and William Callaghan, died 1868 and 1869, aged 2 and 3 years'. It is particularly poignant because a letter survives from W. Callaghan, keeper of the lower lighthouse on Skellig, requesting removal to another station, because he has buried two of his three children on the island and that another was lying ill. Here they are.

Catherine had told us of an extraordinary thing. In a dark corner of one of the seventh-century cells, the same shearwater has hatched its egg each of the past five years. The chick has hatched out the previous day, and it is there with its mother, protected by a piece of netting the wardens have put there. But the most remarkable thing is that Catherine—who is a reliable witness—says she heard the chick cheeping inside the egg before it hatched. She tried to write a poem called 'The Singing Egg'; but whose poem is it, she wondered. The following afternoon I saw several careful children peering in through the dark at the chick which you could just see. Both chick and mother seemed to be entirely impervious to this cautious interest, as if the birds sensed and trusted the goodwill of these entranced watchers. When your eyes adjust to the dark, you can see the mother-bird staring quietly ahead, miles away, deep in thought. We are in good ornithological company here: one of the accompanying poets is Seán Lysaght who is an excellent naturalist as his book *The Clare Island Survey* testifies. Paddy Bushe is pretty good too!

As we come back down at 6.00, the weather is indeed livening up, and we watch the sea roughening spectacularly. After supper we set off westward up the path, past the Guides' huts and the green toilets-on-stilts. One of the guides, Eamon, is strumming a guitar expertly; apparently he is a banjo-player really, but he hasn't got his banjo with him. We go on past him through the gate that leads to the lighthouses. These are extraordinary structures: the New Lighthouse is a wonderfully solid structure from the early nineteenth century with a heavy cast-iron porch brought over from England. How did they build those structures out here? The lighthouse is built of cut granite. It looks exactly like the lighthouse in Finisterre in Galicia which has a cafe and a chillingly mournful bell. Here there is no cafe, though it looks very well appointed inside. It makes you think of 'Flannan Isle' again and that poem's mission "to find out what strange thing might ail / the keepers of the deep sea light". Behind it towards the west is the elegant line of the three Washerwoman Rocks, "tiptoeing away across the waves", in Des Lavelle's lovely phrase. The interior of the main room of the New Lighthouse with its creature comforts can be seen, reconstituted, in the fine Skellig Experience Visitor Centre on Valentia.

The reason why a second, lower lighthouse was built later in the same decade in the 19th century, the 1820s, is a strange one: the Old Lighthouse was high up and got covered by the clouds of the sea mists. The lower light was not visible from so far out but it was below cloud level: just as when you climb inland mountains like The Paps you can look back down through holes in the clouds at the sunlight below. Eamon is an expert climber and his instructions give us confidence at the more vertiginous points. He pats the rock and your foot, saying in his Northern Irish voice "Put her there and you'll be right." (Northern Irish accents always sound reassuring and intelligent, like Scottish ones.) The path up to the Old Lighthouse is seriously precipitous, with breathtaking views down to the sea. The Old Lighthouse is built where the path bends round the north corner before turning to the East behind the monastery to show another view of the Little Skellig. Behind it we walk round to the cliffs above Blue Cove where the dangerous North Landing is. This is the most spectacular and scary point in our day so far. And the same question: how did they get these huge granite blocks up here? It is very melancholy, looking at those rooms shaped and planned for domestic ease, up here, out in the weather.

One of the most remarkable things in the afternoon ascent to the monastery was listening to the storm-petrels calling through the chinks in the stone huts and walls, sounding like that baying noise that toys make when you tilt them forward. We ask Eamon about the return of the pelagic birds in the middle of the night—the petrels and the shearwaters. He says that the shearwaters come back to the big clear rocky space—like a monastic landing-strip—behind the monastery, when it is fully dark. So Seán, Paddy and I set off at 11.00 p.m. with lights, though in this June night we hardly need them. Sure enough though, the petrels are soon flying around our heads more thickly than I have ever seen the bats that the books compare them to. [1] The windy gap at the top is now even scarier; I go through it on all fours. As we

1. "Flight weak and continually fluttering, interspersed with very short periods of gliding: noticeably bat-like, with wingbeats generally rapid". [Footnote: Jim Enticott and David Tipling, *Photographic Handbook : Seabirds of the World*. (London: New Holland Publishers, 1997), 98]

are going along the path towards the flat stone area behind the monastery where we hope to witness the shearwaters, Seán sees one petrel trembling on the path and another one fluttering against the beehive wall like a moth trying to get out a window. They are everywhere, and in every frame of mind, it seems. No wonder the Celtic monks and the Anglo-Saxons thought they were the souls of dead monks and companions.

The fragility and vulnerability of these creatures when they are grounded, with wings spread out like a defeated butterfly, makes it strange to reflect that they belong to the same family as the albatross. And here we are, in mortal danger of injuring them, like the Ancient Mariner. They belong, Enticott tells us, to the family Procellariiformes ('built for the tempest', I suppose) which contains 113 species, varying in size from the smallest Storm-petrel to the huge Royal Albatross: "a weight-difference ratio of some 1:300, not exceeded by any other bird-order" (Enticott-Tipling, 11). It certainly seems as unthinkable to hurt one of these small creatures, out of their element, as to wilfully shoot Coleridge's tutelary albatross in its expansive southern domain. As well as its storm associations, the 'petrel' element in the name is haunting. The derivation is from St. Peter and his impulsive, failed attempt to walk on the water. So the Latin-derived English 'petrel' is matched by the Irish 'peadairín na stoirme' which—fortuitously maybe—introduces the notion of prayer. That notion is certainly not inappropriate on Sceilg Mhichíl. Or is the Irish term 'Mairtineach', as on the stamps? We need Michael Viney! As well as this word, De Bhaldraithe offers us another 'familiar' word for the petrel, 'clampran': a word which Dinneen glosses only as 'one who breeds disunity between people'. I don't know what is going on there. (Dinneen is not at his best on seabirds; I suppose they are not so common around Sliabh Luachra.) The storm-petrel is associated too with the Blessed Virgin, the *mater cara*, from which is derived their other folk-name, 'Mother Carey's Chickens'. Few birds have such a variety of associations.

We sat in the wind at the top and waited, but we didn't find the dark, silent swish of the returning shearwaters that Paddy had witnessed twenty years ago when he stayed overnight on the hard floor of one of the beehive huts. Apparently their return is less certain on fine nights like this. But as we were picking our way back down, all the time taking care not to tread on the cowering petrels which took no evasive action, we heard a different, more clucking, ratcheting voice from the burrows at our feet. That may have been the nesting shearwaters, but it may also have been a variant of the puffin call. When we shone a light on the puffins, they just stood there blankly, like dazzled rabbits. When we got back down we discovered that Eamon had found a shearwater on the path by the huts and shown it to Cathal Ó Searcaigh, the affable fourth member of our group who had declined the offer to climb the 600 steps into the windy darkness. Then bed in my wonderful hut-refuge, listening to the sea and the incessant, soul-like calling of the birds. As I fall asleep, I am resisting, fearing that the loss of consciousness will break the connexion with this extraordinary day.

Weather

Eight miles off the coast, you are that much
nearer the weather, in an element
where the seabirds dwell in their daily round.
You take your post on watch. There is nothing.
And then, poor sleep-craving disciple,
you wake to see what the Wanderer found,
all around you: sailors' spirits
who bring there not many known songs.
Dark invisible, inaudible
winged souls, peopling the dark above your head.

The weather next morning has changed indeed: the sea has turned grey and turbulent with a strong south-east wind. No boats today, as Eoin had predicted. You inevitably think of the 8th or 9th-century Irish poem from the margins of a Swiss manuscript from St. Gall, about the roughness of the sea acting as protection by being impassable for the Viking predators.

> The wind tonight is bitter,
> it tousles the sea's white hair;
> I have no fear that gentle seas
> will bring fierce warriors from Norway.
> (Trans. Ruth P.M. Lehmann, 1982, p.62)

Will there be boats tomorrow when I am due to return to examining duties in Oxford? Would I like there to be? Beneath my window the white waves are crashing on the rock where the stories say the Vikings pinned down the abbot and left him to die. The puffin is pulling his starter-drawstring outside my window; now I do photograph it, and a very bedraggled figure it cuts. Paddy and I walk down to the landing-stage which is being fiercely threshed by the sea. I ring Oxford from the helipad at the landing-stage—the only place you can get reception—and discover that it is oppressively hot and thunder-threatened there. I come back to the hut, watching brilliant seas and guillemots and gannets. In the afternoon we walk halfway up to the monastery as the weather worsens: rain, wind and swollen sea. We go down to Blind Man's Cove where we are shown guillemot and kittiwake chicks on the ledge by Maggie, the young OPW guide from Castleisland who is a friend of neighbours of ours in Cullen. She is an archaeologist, but she has an impressive, unfailing knowledge of the distinctions between the birds, by species and gender.

After the squalls and storms of the day, and spaghetti supper in Paddy's hut, there follows a spectacular clearance: a beautifully sunny and windy evening, followed by a gibbous moon behind the Wailing Woman. The impression of this worn cross—disturbing at the best of times—has gained a new grimness by its resemblance now to the tortured, electrode-wearing figure from Abu Ghraib. But at 11.30 Sean and Catherine dance on the small space in front of her, with a hundred-feet drop and the Little Skellig behind them. The puffins and I can hardly watch. Fewer petrels tonight, and the day—or night—ends watching the kittiwakes and razorbills on the black ledges of Blind Man's Cove again.

Next morning—Monday 29th of June—is the day of the Scattering, as it is called at Puck Fair. But will we be able to scatter? I have spent a momentous-feeling restless night, hearing the haunting bird-calls being drowned out by the wind and the waves. I have morning dreams of wrecked and half-rebuilt houses, featuring one of our Cullen neighbours with no face and a hole for a mouth, like the carving of Envy at Blythburgh in Suffolk. Then we get up into a brilliant, sunny, windy morning. More photographs of the Little Skellig which looks differently brilliant and expressive in every hour, light and weather. Behind it we watch the boats setting out from Portmagee: Des Lavelle first; but if one goes, they all go. Sure enough, several boatloads of visitors arrive to invade our private realm, and we climb to the monastery with them. We hear Maggie amidst the beehives give a compelling and learned account of the monastic remains to a rapt international audience that she addresses as 'ye', making me reflect as I often do what a lamentable loss to Standard English that friendly, distinctive plural form was. Or maybe we were all just charmed by Maggie from Castleisland.

And after lunch we take to the boats. At the tricky landing-stage I manage to drop into the sea Seán's book which he was giving to Cathal. The author takes it in excellent part, saying its presence in these waters is a good omen, presaging our return, like the coins in the Trevi Fountain in Rome. Then an exhilarating voyage back with Eoin in the orange boat. Again there is a dog with a lolling tongue, staring over the side and fancying his chances with the guillemots. Maggie's boy-friend from Ballydesmond is on the boat, and he and I talk about common acquaintances, like in Percy French's 'Emigrant's Letter'.

The Skellig Listeners

Even at eleven o'clock when we looked out
it was not dark enough that summer night
to prompt them to their silent return
from the pelagic deep. So we waited
until midnight before we made the climb
to our monastery vigil. Still we didn't
catch them in the act. Then suddenly
we knew they were there: that they had somehow,
no pace perceived, filled the night above our heads
with big wings, and yes, the shearwater calls
were all around us. Just as wonderful,
every gap in the stone Beehive walls
was filled with the sound of petrels,
disconnected from their vocal chords
like grasshopper or snipe. Going back down
we had to be careful not to stand on them
where they shrank back into the rock
that they'd been natives of for aeons before us.

࿇

We come back into Portmagee, with the sun still shining on it, and now we see the restored monastic buildings on Illaunloughan with a mixture of awe and guilt at not recognising its significance as a premonition on the way out less than three days before. A miniature lifetime seems to have passed in the interim. It was hard to know what to talk about as we had a drink in the pub in Portmagee. Casual talk of this and that, as Yeats calls it, did not measure up to the scenes and sounds and creatures we had been among for three days. My account has been bird-slanted: not just because it is the birds to whom the great rocks now primarily belong, but also because of the absentees who can be sensed nearly as fully as the birds who have stayed on as their representatives: the monks who gave the place a meaning which we still try to receive with our cruder modern antennae. Our return had been carefully planned of course: we hadn't set off without a compass, trusting in the love of God. But we have been on pilgrimage. We understand now the extraordinary choice that those monks and seafarers made, and how much nobler a choice it was than anything that we could opt for: we have glimpsed the world experienced by the Egyptian Desert Fathers who said "Except a man shall say in his heart I alone and God are in this world he shall not find peace"[2]. However we put it, and whatever we understand by God, it is the same truth we are grasping, as it has been expressed down the ages. Matthew Arnold used it as a metaphor:

> Yes! In the sea of life enisled,
> With echoing straits between us thrown,
> Dotting the shoreless watery wild,
> We mortal millions live *alone*.

How much grander was the Seafarer's and the Skellig hermit's literal enactment of that pilgrimage!

2. [Quoted in *High Island* by Jenny White Marshall and Grellan D. Rourke. Duchas: Town House and Country House Dublin, 2000, p.1: the beautiful sister-book of the *Hidden Hermitage* above]

Cathal Ó Searcaigh

Oíche den dá oíche a chaith mé ar an Sceilg i dtrátha na Féile Eoin i mbliana, tháinig manach chugam i mo chodladh, fear óg, caol ard in aibíd dhonn scaoilte, cochall manaigh ar a cheann. Níor mhothaigh mé aon eagla ina láthair. Bhí sé gnaoiúil ina dhreach agus grástúil ina chuid gluaiseachtaí. Shuígh sé ag colbha na leapa agus d'fhéach orm go geanúil.

"Mé Tuathal Mac Liag, file," adúirt sé i gcanúint bhinn nár chuala mé a macasamhail ariamh. "Anois, de réir mar a chluinim, níl trácht ar mo shaothar i laoi ná i litir. Dá bhithín sin … "

D'fhéach sé orm go géar amhail is le rá go raibh sé de dhualgas orm teanga a thabhairt don tost seo a thit ar a shaothar. Sin a tuigeadh dom ar scor ar bith.

"Ba mhór mo spéis i bhfearaibh ach bhí mo chroí istigh i gCaomhán, mo bhráthair sa tír úd thall."

Leis sin scread éan uaigneach éigin amuigh i ndeireadh na hoíche agus dhúisigh mé i dtobainne as mo chodladh. Bhí mo mhanach imithe is an lá ag breacadh, cáitheadh liath na maidne ar an mhuir mhóir os coinne na fuinneoige. Ghoill sé orm nach raibh ár gcaidreamh níos dlúithe. Bhí cumhaidh orm i ndiaidh an té seo a tháinig chugam as an tsaol eile … as an tsamhlaíocht … níl fhios agam! Ó shoin i leith tá na dánta seo ag fabhrú i m'aigne …

Sa Mhainistir

Géag ar ghéag ár gcual cnámh
á mheilt is á mhionú sa chré mhéith;
ár mbunadh romhainn a chreid go tréan
gan focal astu anois faoi ghlóir Mhic Dé.

During one of the two nights I spent on Skellig around Saint John's Day this year, a monk came to me in my sleep, a young slender man in a brown, loosened habit, with a cowl on his head. I felt no fear in his presence. His expression was kindly and his movements graceful. He sat on the edge of the bed, and spoke affectionately to me.

"I am Tuathal Mac Liag, a poet," he said, in a pleasant dialect I had never before heard. "Now, as I understand it, my work is unknown to the written word. And so … "

He looked keenly at me, as if to say that I had a duty to break the silence that had fallen on his work. In any case, that is what I understood.

"I was greatly drawn to men, but my heart was embedded in Caomhán, my brother across the sea."

Just then some bird screeched out in the end of the night, and I awoke abruptly from my sleep. My monk had disappeared, dawn was breaking, and grey morning drizzled on the wide sea outside my window. It upset me that our conversation had not gone deeper. I missed this person who had come to me from the otherworld … from the imagination … from wherever! Ever since, these poems have been taking shape in my mind …

In the Monastery

Limb upon limb our mound of bones
is milled and ground beneath the sod;
our forefathers, once loud in their belief,
are silent now on the glory of God.

Ceathrúintí Thuathal Mac Liag

1.

Mé Tuathal Mac Liag
 file fann na Sceilge;
Rófhada mé anseo
 ag cothú ceilge

Idir an ceann teann
 is an croí lag.
Briost liom an t-oileán
 is mo shaol lom

I ndíseartan gaoithe
 i bhfad ó mo ghaol:
Caomhán óg aoibhálainn,
 leannán slatchaol.

2.

I gcathair chrábhaidh Chiaráin
 atá sé, cois na habhna;
áitreamh réidh na gréine,
 glé os cionn na Sionna.

Aoibhinn liom an cruinntheach
 i gclós úd na gceall;
Ansiúd a phógfainn Caomhán …
 Á! dá mbéinnse sall.

Tuathal Mac Liag's Quatrains

1.

I am Tuathal Mac Liag
 the silent poet of Skellig;
too long I'm out here
 plotting mischief

between the hot head
 and the faint heart.
The island revolts me,
 this world apart

in a windwhipped retreat
 remote from affection:
Caomhán, young and smiling,
 my lover, willow-slender.

2.

He's in Ciarán's holy city,
 the riverside monastery
where the sun scatters plenitude,
 bright above the Shannon.

I love the rounded stone
 cells of that enclosure;
it's there I'd kiss Caomhán …
 oh! just to go there!

Imíonn caitheamh is baol
    ar gach uile dhúil
ach go dtaga lá m'éaga
    eisean mo mhian súl.

I ndíthreabh fuar siúlaim
    ar chonair nach cóir,
Ní ag feacadh glún ach ag cumadh
    laoithe cumainn ina onóir.

"Ná bac an domhan, a mhanaigh,
    is gheobhair Ríocht Dé";
ach in éagmais mo ghaol fola
    níl Neamh ar bith gan é.

3.

Ní domhsa slí an tSoiscéil
    ná síorghuí an Rí;
b'aoibhneas domhsa i gcónaí
    dreabhlas dí agus suirí.

Ní fhanaim ag canadh
    sailm na dtráth;
nó ag naomhadh an anama
    i gcóir lá an bhrátha.

na mianta a shatailt go dian
    roimh dul i ndáil báis
ní háil liom. B'uaisle i bhfad
    síothlú i bhfeis máis …

Decay and slow attrition
> overtake every being
but until my dying hour
> he is all I long to see.

Around a cold hermitage
> I walk an uneven way,
not genuflecting, but creating
> verses in his praise!

"Monk, abjure the world,
> to attain to God's kingdom";
but without my closest love
> there cannot be a heaven.

3.

Not for me the way of Scripture
> or endless, endless praying;
my enjoyment ever
> was wine and lovemaking.

For psalms at appointed hours
> I do not stop to pray;
neither do I sanctify
> my soul for judgment day.

To trample down desire
> before the face of death
is not for me. Better to expire
> in a festival of flesh.

Sásaigh do mhian sa tsaol—
    gheibhid na huile bás—
is ón uair go bhfuil an úir tharat
    ní bhfaighid grásta nó spás.

4.

Oileán lom na dtonn,
    tearmann Talcheann;
beag is fiú de mhaith ann,
    cothú garbh gann.

Tréanas géir an léin,
    tionól dochma bréan;
beag an baol teaspúlacht …
    Éalód as thar aigéan.

Ord ná riail ná cuing cléire
    ní choisceoidh mo rith;
chugatsa, a chroí, de rúide treise …
    deise liom tú ná Dia ar bith.

Satisfy your lust for life—
>   death comes to everyone,
and when your hour for earthing comes
>   all scope, all grace, are gone.

   4.

This stark, this wave-bound island,
>   Táilcheann's sanctuary;
little good it was to him
>   poor, scarce sustenance.

The cutting strength of sorrow,
>   a woeful congregation;
no flesh will ever sing here …
>   I'll dare the ocean.

Order, rule or clerical yoke
>   will not obstruct my run
to you, dear heart, with utmost speed …
>   God is not. You're the one.

Tuathal ag Cuimhneamh ar Chaomhán

Buí, buí do chneas
    a chroí;
        buí deas an fhómhair
i dteas na gcnoc.

Tá lí na gréine, lí
    na seirce
        ag apú na heornan
i ngort d'uchta.

Tá an grán buí
    ag fás
        go tiubh agus go fras
i mám do mhása.

Is geal liom do bhuí
    san oíche;
        buí cumhra an arbhair
ag teacht i gcraobh

i d'aoibh, buí teasaí
    an fhómhair
        ag cur lasair i do chéadfaí.
A bhuí duitse, a chroí,

is fear faobhair mé
    anocht;
        an buanaí a thig chugat
cruaidh agus tarnocht.

Tuathal Daydreams Caomhán

Amber, amber your skin,
    dear heart;
        a harvest amber
in hillside heat.

The sun's tongue, the tongue
    of love
        ripens the barley
that furrows your breast.

The amber grain
    is growing
        rampant, abundant,
in the cleft of your cheeks.

Your amber brightens
    my night;
        the perfumed amber of barley
coming to fruit

in your smile, the glowing amber
    of harvest-time
        lighting your senses.
In your ambience, dear heart,

I am edged steel
    tonight;
        the reaper who comes to you
tempered, naked.

Tuathal ag Mealladh Chaomháin

Tá nathair bheo
    an cheo
        ag lúbarnach
chugainn ó riasc na gcorr.

Tá úll órbhuí
    na gealaí
        ag apú
go meallacach os ár gcionn.

Mór an tsuáilce
    duáilce
        a dhéanamh leatsa
i gclúid úr na gcraobh.

Íosfaimid an t-úll,
    ceansóidh muid
        an nathair.
Ní bheidh tú ina aithreachas

Anois nó go deo.
    Níl Dia ar bith
        anseo
le smál a chur ar ár n-aoibhneas.

Tuathal Seduces Caomhán

The living serpent
      of the mist
           twists
towards us from the herons' bog.

The gilded apple
      of the moon
           ripens into
temptation over our heads.

It's pure joy
      to be impure
           with you
stretched under the branches.

We will eat the apple,
      we will confound
           the serpent
with no contrition, no fatherly forgiveness

now or forever.
      God is neither
           here nor there
to corrupt our joy.

Paidir Thuathail

Ár n-athair atá ar Neamh
    go ndearmadfar d'ainm is nach dtaga
    do ríocht. Ar a bhfaca tú ariamh
Ná tar inar láthair. Tá go leor againn
den ghlóir is den bhriathar, den dallamhullóg dhiaga.
    Fan ansiúd i do chlúid
    áit a bhfuil an saol ar do thoil agat.
Ná buair tú féin linne,
Ní dhéanfá ach muid a chur faoi smúid.
    Tá ár sáith os ár gcoinne
    gan a bheith go síoraí faoi do thoilse.
Ár n-arán laethúil, soláthróidh muid é
inniu agus gach aon lá eile.
    Ní chreideann muid i d'fhéile.
    Ar son Dé ná tóg orainn ár n-easpa céille—
Tá cathú orainn gur tharla sé—
ach muid féin a chruthaigh tú
    agus inár gcosúlacht féin, arú!
    Maith dhúinn do chionta
mar a mhaithimid duitse ár gcionta féin.
Saor sinn ó do chráifeacht
    is saoróidh sinne tusa ó bhreall ár ndiagantachta.
    Móraigh an dia ionainne
is móróidh muidinne an duine ionatsa
tré shaol na saol, Áiméan.

Tuathal's Prayer

Our Father, who art in Heaven,
    forgotten be thy name, and never
      may thy kingdom come. In the name of creation
come not amongst us. We have had enough
of the glorious word, the deistic deceit.
    Rest in thine own comfort
      and live according to thine own will.
Trouble not thyself with us;
Thou wouldst merely leave us under a cloud.
    We have tribulations enough
      without thine eternal jurisdiction
Our daily bread, we will provide
today, and the rest of our days.
    We do not trust in thy beneficence.
      For God's sake, begrudge us not our foolishness—
we do repent of it—
but we ourselves created thee
    and, believe it or not, in our own likeness!
    Forgive us thy trespasses
as we forgive thee our trespasses.
Deliver us from thy piety
    and we will deliver thee from our theological delusions.
    Exalt the divine in us
and we will exalt the human in thee
forever and ever. Amen.

Macdara Woods

Timesis

But O the Chevalier Baldassare
Who had fierce O such fierce tremors!
At Assisi they say it happened.
Joseph grabbed him by the hair
Wheeled him round in aether
And from the brightness of the air
Set him down safe O untrembling.
   —John Jordan, from 'The Flying Men'

On the 13th of May 2009, around eleven in the morning, I fell on a moving staircase at Leonardo Da Vinci airport, Fiumicino, doing myself severe injury. I had been unwell in the spring and was now on my way to Umbria with laptop and notebooks, but above all with time, to work on completing a new book of poems. And ancillary to that to revisit properly the material arising out of my three magical days and nights of engagement with the stone steps of Sceilg Mhichíl in June 2008.

I was the only one on the moving stairs to the train ticket office, travelling sedately up, congratulating myself on how easily things were going, when suddenly, about half way to the top, I found myself flying backward, for no reason that I can tell, in a slow-motion arc through empty air to the bottom. I was fully conscious of the danger of the hard sharpness of the moving edges of the steps and tried to protect my head and spine as I fell, but landed heavily on my right shoulder at the bottom, breaking my collarbone into four separate pieces and also breaking five ribs. Nobody had seen what happened it seemed, nor had it registered on any CCTV apparently, there was no outcry, the steps kept moving and I was carried up once more—twisted in a heap as I had landed, with all my belongings about me—to the top where I rolled off and half sat half lay with my back against a low wall.

The immediate feeling was shock, being totally stunned and winded, and then acute pain and helplessness; hit by the realisation that for the first time in my life I could simply go no further under my own direction. There was no question of waiting quietly until I got my breath back, no way I could limp or crawl or escape from this: something bad had happened. I was broken.

Like that bleak imperative *briathar saor*, half-way through, of the *Maldon* Anglo-Saxon fragment—*brocen wurde*.

I saw a man looking at me; I made a sign and he came over. He asked what the matter was and I told him I had fallen on the moving staircase. He disapppeared and came back with an off-duty medical person who told me I had probably dislocated my shoulder and that I would be taken to hospital. Then, at last, as the official link in the chain of events, a professionally sceptical woman in a peaked cap arrived from Security.

If I get you an ambulance, she said, you'll have to pay.
Which provoked a blast of outraged indignation from the gathering crowd. How can you ask an injured person to pay? demanded one. I apologise for Italy, declared another.

Call one anyhow, I told her, I'm insured.

An ambulance crew arrived at once and took me to the emergency room of the hospital 20 kilometres away at spectacular speed, swaying around on my stretcher with all my baggage swaying about me and without any mention of money at all. In fact that Security woman at the top of the escalator was the only person who mentioned money or payment throughout the whole affair.

The initial doctor was kind, careful and efficient. He first diagnosed the broken bone and strapped me into a harness explaining it was to hold my shoulders back, ("now begins your crucifixion"), gave me a genuinely efficacious pain killer to take on the spot and another in a glass phial to have by me. Fortunately, as it turned out later. And when the X-rays showed that a number of ribs were broken as well as the clavicle, the same doctor saw me through a CAT scan to make sure there was no further internal damage and then returned me on my trolley to a kind of general holding ward.

That evening as his shift was ending he came to see me where I was lying, to tell me how things were, that I would be staying the night, in some other section perhaps, until Eiléan could pick me up the following day as had been arranged by phone. But when the night shift marched in to take command, led by another doctor arrayed in green scrubs and sporting a head of permed red hair, things took a sinister tilt.

Who is this person with a broken clavicle? he demanded eventually.

I identified myself.

Well you can leave. I'm letting you go.

Where? said I.

Home, said he, with a private kind of smile, which seemed out of place to me since it was clear that I was a foreigner, in transit.

But the other doctor, I began carefully, aware of sensitive boundaries, the other doctor, whom I first saw, said I'd be staying the night ... until my wife arrives from Dublin tomorrow.

Sono Io Il Dottore, he interrupted, *Sono Io Il Dottore*, and I knew that I was caught up in a demarcation feud.

I am a sixty-seven year old man, I said, a foreigner. I have been travelling since six-thirty this morning. I am in great pain and distress and the nearest home to me is Umbria.

To which he replied that there was no shortage of hotels in Rome.

So at nine-thirty at night, after tripartite argument between the *dottore* and me and Eiléan on my mobile, I was delivered into the care of a random taxi driver—who turned out to be an angel in effect, first protesting on my behalf, then finding me a sane and welcoming hotel nearby on the seafront, where I went to my room, levered off the neck of the medicine phial left-handedly in the keyhole of the wardrobe, held the liquid under my tongue for a minute as instructed, then swallowed it, not caring whether it contained bits of glass or not, and lay down. Broken, alone, helpless, severely disabled and in appalling agony.

Eiléan arrived early the following afternoon in a hired car, from the airport, and drove me to Umbria, where I stayed through the rest of the summer, recuperating. And I worked at it: exercising the arm, hand and shoulder, swimming eventually and riding a bicycle, walking six ground-level kilometres every day up and down the yard and trying to return to the work-zone, the place where real things happen; trying to rediscover the avenues of thought I had brought with me, or even to form new patterns or points of departure, somehow to get back to where I had been, from whatever direction.

But this proved to be impossible. The realisation of being broken that had first hit me as I lay on the floor at the top of the escalator grew over the summer months, for all my work, for all the reassurance from the solicitous doctors in Perugia, there was no way in which I could resume what I had been doing, and above all no sign of that essential intuitive leap of the heart for which I was desperately waiting. Something had been destroyed and what memories did drift in from before the break were unalive and undirected.

And as it turned out the bones—apart from the ribs—had not healed at all, had not knit inside the large accumulation of callus. Now there is an unhealed gap of two centimetres in my shoulder, and my right side is dropping. My arm, shoulder and upper back are constantly painful, I am partly disabled, and bar slowly signing my name and inscribing short lists I effectively cannot write by hand. As I type this I am waiting for an operation to put the unhealed process right by means of a graft of living bone from my hip.

Notes from June 2008

The arrival itself was all by air. And that is what most remains with me: the verticality of it all.

Flying across the plain of Ireland, coming down into Kerry, bacon and eggs in the pub in Portmagee, and then the boat ride over.

Always sailing between sea and sky, the great rolling meadows of the sea, where one might wish to walk. The mad desire to throw one leg over the side of the boat, step down and walk across the surface of the sea.

[But of course we don't, as in airports we follow the arrows, askew and Janus-strange as Orpheus in the underworld.

Mem: The Graduate Student in Cervantes who believed himself to be made out of glass and walked in the middle of the street in order to avoid falling roof-tiles.
Cotard's Syndrome]

To skim over the sea as birds do, as I did as a child, when I walked across the grassy surface of the earth.

Romanesco Island.

[Once in a restaurant by Lake Trasimeno, I saw strange underwater creatures brought to the neighbouring table ...]

Up ahead, the islands. Cathedrals. Like two of Stalin's gothic sisters rising knee-deep out of Moscow. The romanesco strangeness of the Little Sceilg, sea-vegetable, lunar underwater, underwater lunar,(pastoral historical tragical): gannets wheeling lazily perpetually around it like lazy midges.

Guillemots, razorbills ...

[Lunar with bird droppings, guano white, the alkali desert south of Albacete, the Exemplary Tales again and those southern Spanish salt flats in the sun].

How the sun shone for three days? That we landed light as dragon flies, and that Leonard Cohen was singing in a downpour in far-off Dublin?

Narrow lighthouse road, nineteenth century blasting, marks of drilled charge-holes on the side.

[The first station   Above where we slept in the OPW hut.

Everything here is above. The rock rears above us, we are above the sea, the sea is above the depths. The depths above us by mirror magic. Mythology.

I walked up to the crying woman before dawn   the sun rising over Ireland to the east of me   so clear you could see the whole way to Cork   the long low light coming from the east   to light the west   Sunrise but then that evening   light from the west   the crying woman backlit hair flying in the solar wind]

*seeing and being (part of) (seeing)
the sunrise / son an island
groaning with birds*

steps everywhere   a maze of steps   climbing through a state of mind   and at the top the (not Greek) polis   city-state   a European paradigm   cathedral and city   polis set on a buttress all set on a shoulder

*[The beehive cells
On the outside huge*

How matter of fact
The puffins and fulmars

The sun above the little sceilg
On which
The windows are fixed
How inclusive these islands are
More
Inclusive than inward

Ships (sail-boat) (inward turned)
Turned to look
For a moment (to look)
Their purpose interrupted

Puffins
With the faces of Marcel Marceau

On the lighthouse path alone
At night
The(y) moan and groan within
The fabric of the rock

((And the panting
Of a dog who isn't there))]

[weight of stone
and yet how light it looks
laid out so in slabs

that flowing present
stone
stone waterfalls
slow cataracts
cascades

stone cadences
caduti

gothic high cathedral
floating
upon all of this (the odd being right)
sheer mountain top
(and all the layers
of vessels overhead)
(full) ninety fathoms deep

at the summit there is urban
the citta ideale
devoid of people
quartz paved squares

far below the surface
all that scrabbling life
support of faith
(belief) for flying men
and when a wall gives way
we fill it in
and start again

❧

Steps: it was the steps of the escalator   the moving staircase
that did for me
Unable to return   among the flying men   to   the place where
I did not fall

❧

The steps of Sceilg Mhichíl are an amazement. A drunkenness of steps akin to the drunkenness of the deeps. Never before have I been so conscious of stone, layers of stone, reshaped stone reset into the very stone from which it has been cut. Appearing to become lighter and lighter until it is all a weight-bearing filigree of engineering, a functional lattice-work of improbability. The whole orientation has become upward, like a rocket, and yet strangely horizontal; you find you are not looking up or down but are instead inside a perspective giving outward at an impossible 360 degree angle, at one with sea and sky, flying. Everything is flying, people, birds, buttresses of stone, clouds, and a school of Risso dolphins in the sea below.

How can it be? The swelling chambers of the heart, the strain on the knees; it is all shoring and wall, and untouched rock with loose surface soil of pinks, sea campion and sea spinach, of sphagnum moss and wind and birds. The only way to deal with it is to become part of it and in so becoming we begin to realise other dimensions of breathlessness as we toil upwards bent over, nose to stone, begin to see the zig-zag paths of ancient steps as antic in themselves, young frisky oxygenated walls, or—credible enough in this landscape of primaeval untouched slabs—as walls that have simply taken to walking about.

Up the first and second sections, past the Crying Woman, swinging about across the haunch of hill slope and then past the dog-leg turn, sharp as a hare's change of direction pursued by hounds, up through a different orientation to the grassy space on the saddle and, from there, like the sudden shocking primal invitation of Courbet's *Origine du Monde* on the wall of the Musée d'Orsay, the almost-last stretch of steps that seem to hang suspended, swaying almost, on an invisible chain anchored by wind-carved pillars of rock, and then the final reach up to the unseen place above. The little garden enclave, the beehive cells that seem so big, so much an elemental shape, a shape only, until you become aware of, and enter into, the sheer urban cohesion of it, in the same way as when you enter into one of those walled Italian hill-towns that from below look as tight and impregnable as an oyster.

Because this place is also a statement, designed to be seen from below, built out of time and stone, the same permanence / impermanence of the great gothic spires, which may or may not fall down: but which—if they do—will be rebuilt again. The multi-terracing behind impressive cut-stone city-walls, orchestrated approaches, the aligned positioning of one cell doorway in relation to another, the purposeful direction of sewage waste into a huge cleft in the rocks to the abyss below, rain water saved from grooves in the rock collected by a filter system into two wells or cisterns; all of these speak of the give and take of cohabitation, the unseen but unmistakable ways in which cities function.

What I found myself recognising, and still do thinking back on it, was the inherited awareness and civic purpose epitomised in that most basic and essential of all urban areas, the common public space. The place where human scale and preoccupations are respected. And there it was, in three-hundred-and-fifty-million-year-old stone, on top of this most westerly statement of an urban-hermit European spirit: clear to see, the purple-quartz-paved open square. This was not the same as visiting, say, the extraordinary clifftop Franciscan eyrie of cells and church cut huddling into the rockface at Greccio, but a planned conurbation of buildings, with church and garden and graveyard and levels and public squares. And air and ocean. A space for living long-term, for living with, and in spite of, the foibles of others. One solution to the recurring question of how two or more human organisms can share a common patch of ground.

For all my working on high buildings in London in the sixties I do not have a good head for heights, but for a moment there in that small paved space I had a glimpse of, a feeling of being there at, the start of things, as too I sometimes had on high flat rooves on construction sites in Swiss Cottage and Shepherd's Bush. A rush of awareness and apprehension mixed up with wind and dizziness, a feeling of momentary completeness, of being one again with the Flying Men, the figure of the diver in the painted tombs in the Etruscan city of the dead at Tarquinia, the rocks where they held the Council on the Acropolis, the flowing levels of Delphi, pictures of the cascading walls of Lhasa, the Basilica of Assisi rising from the Umbrian plain, the marble square of Salamanca in the dawn, the Casas Colgadas suspended like folded sleeping bats in Cuenca, floating Gubbio and the wolf and the Festa of the Ceri, the ascendant Dome of the Rock in Jerusalem, the image of the hanging gardens of Babylon, all the countless man-made heavier-than-air terraces and platforms and the open squares supported by them.

While taking part in a symposium on the subject of Home Lands on the island of Paros a few years ago, I found myself wondering had I somehow in my life come to lose the village, had I misread Genesis, somehow become separated from myself? I do know that I was granted a glimpse of my poem in that inner walled enclosure of human endeavour and forbearance high above the ocean, a stone Eden garden of the air, and that I tried to carry it with me, and that I lost it, appropriately enough, in the Fall on the staircase and the business of survival and reassemblage. After such a dislocation things start anew, if we are lucky, but that's the Faustian catch: things start anew, they do not pick up and continue. There is a kind of enforced *timesis*, like electroconvulsive therapy or the French Revolution, wonderful or terrible depending on who is speaking.

This is part of a particular existential problem as stated by Seamus Heaney at the Kavanagh centenary celebrations in Inniskeen in 2004: the poet has to make the poem, see it into existence; and then has to do the whole thing over again, but differently. I wrote about the pain letting go, I wrote about my reduced conscious world being anchored by a hole in the daytime window-shutter. I wrote about walking later up and down the yard and the system of red and white clothes-pegs I had worked out to measure the distance covered: let 20 pegs equal one kilometre. I wrote about seeing things anew and yet recognising them. And in the end, in a way, I found myself, albeit imperfectly, back onto a kind of parallel track to, a cousin at several long removes from, where I had been.

The painting of the *Citta Ideale*, in the National Gallery of the Marche in Urbino, has always fascinated me: the painted marble city, laid out in public areas of human scale, a perfection of perspectives but with no living visible creature in it. And when I was on the move again, poetically and every other way, it became a kind of visual mantra to my travelling. I picked up on echoes of the Sceilg in the palladian squares of Vicenza, and in a performance of *Andromache* I saw there in the Teatro Olimpico, another kind of open public place. I was on my way to Venice, and I felt it again and again in ten days walking around that city of seascapes and islands, through narrow streets and narrower passageways, from bridge to bridge, always from one square leading to another.

Because I read it in Venice I appreciated all the more the truth of Calvino's *Imaginary Cities:* that all of them in the end are the same city. Enough to be able to finish my own book, more or less; enough to have met again with Miz Moon, late of Ephesus and Delphi, Collateral of Bríd and Doinn. The fact that I have not written the particular poem I glimpsed on the Sceilg does not mean that I never will: the path to any poem can be more zig-zag than the steps on that extraordinary rock, the point of arrival the same. Touch one ocean and you touch them all. I know that I was possessed there for a long moment, as by a slow air, and that the possession remains alive inside me still, despite my being broken on the Roman steps. Meanwhile, we continue searching:

In the Light of Whipple's Moon

My first time travelling
With Ms Jackie Smith
She had but lately changed
From being a silver birch
Become a silver beech

On six-inch high stilettos
Containing within her
A continent of knowledge
And she a fleet of bark canoes
To sail the waters

Next I saw her in midwinter
In the mountains
Standing with open arms
And upthrust branches
Eloquent against the sky

In what she called
Her stance for taking off
And where are we aiming for
I asked what next? Still
Travelling light enough

To fly through light itself
She said—to get from here
To the nearest star
Or near enough to touch
Starts with a ten-day walk

Leaving the *case sparse*
Scattered houses on your left
Over the land of olives
Across the icy lake of moons
To reach the scattered disc

But first you have to learn
Perhaps by telescope
The names and constellations
Of vanished peoples
In the maproom of the Doge

All that Magnificence
Scrolled dolphins reading books
And Chiron with a dorsal fin
Turned arabesque
Ambiguous below the waist

Remember what she said
The Delphic priestess on the rock
The words before she struck
The downward stroke
That left you broken up

Once more you must move on
Align the Omphalos
Just play it as it lays my dear
And after that who knows—
The centre of the universe?

—Macdara Woods
January 2010

At the Butler Arms

*No boats this week, too choppy, so we watch
from a spread table beneath
a Charlie Chaplin photograph
who often came here for a holiday;
or we drive over to Finian's Cove to study
the eight-mile stretch*

*of water between here and Sceilig Mhichíl
where the old anchorites
and monks who chose the place and raised
a church, two chapels and six drystone huts,
survived on dulse and mackerel
out in the haze.*

*No pleasant woodland there, no grazing deer
such as the others knew
above fly-bubbling salmon streams ashore
in field and forest beneath oak and yew—
not calm, contemplative ease
but violent seas.*

*Six hundred years of plainchant and response,
gannets and cormorants; six
centuries of the 'crude bronze crucifix'
in Finian's church, wine cup and canticle,
prayer book and reading candle,
thistles, sea-campions.*

How could you get inside their bony heads?
Wrapped up in mystic mists,
they spent the hours and years
wrestling with the hot flesh in their cold beds,
their backs to Europe and the wars,
talking to ghosts.

What news of the great world, of Gaul and Rome,
Iona and Cappadocia? Some,
but late; prostrate at Easter in the nave
they listened to the whistling wave
and saw the sun sink in an infinite ocean
world of its own.

Strong winds continue, so no trip this time.
Still, it could be predictable to climb
to the immense height and the whole shocking
reach of the Atlantic (with special care
since there's no handrail there).
No going back,

is there, to that wild hush of dedication,
to the solitude, the intense belief,
the last rock of an abandoned civilization
whose dim lights glimmered in a distant age
to illuminate at the edge
a future life.

—Derek Mahon

Notes on Contributors

PADDY BUSHE was born in Dublin in 1948. He has lived in Waterville, Co. Kerry since 1973 and has been visiting Skellig Michael, with increasing regularity, ever since. He writes in both English and Irish and has published eight volumes of poetry, the most recent of which are *Gile na Gile* (Coiscéim, 2006) and *To Ring in Silence: New and Selected Poems* (Dedalus, 2008), a bilingual volume. He has also published three books of translation (from Irish, Scottish Gaelic and Chinese). He has won the Listowel Poetry Prize, The Michael Hartnett Award, Duais Filíochta an Oireachtais, and the Strokestown International Poetry Prize. A member of Aosdána, he is currently working on a study of the cultural landscape of Iveragh.

JOHN F. DEANE was born on Achill Island 1943. He founded Poetry Ireland and *Poetry Ireland Review* in 1979. He has published several collections of poetry and some fiction. He has won the O'Shaughnessy Award for Irish Poetry, the Marten Toonder Award for Literature and poetry prizes from Italy and Romania and been shortlisted for both the T.S. Eliot prize and The Irish Times Poetry Now Award. His most recent poetry collection is *A Little Book of Hours* (Carcanet, 2008). He is a member of Aosdána. In 2007 the French Government honoured him by making him 'Chevalier de l'ordre des arts et des lettres'. In 2008 he was visiting scholar in the Burns Library of Boston College. Blackstaff Press will publish, in October 2010, a new novel, *Where No Storms Come,* and in December Columba Press will publish a book of essays, *The Works of Love.* His next poetry collection, *Eye of the Hare,* will come from Carcanet in June 2011.

THEO DORGAN is a poet, prose writer, editor and documentary scriptwriter. His most recent publications are *What This Earth Cost Us* (2008) and *Greek* (2010), both from Dedalus Press who earlier this year reissued *Sailing for Home,* his acclaimed prose account of a transatlantic voyage from the Caribbean to his native Cork. The follow-up volume, *Time on the Ocean,* which chronicles a journey through the South Atlantic under sail, was published in late 2010 by New Island. He is a member of

Aosdána and is the 2010 recipient of the Lawrence O'Shaughnessy Award for Irish Poetry (USA).

KERRY HARDIE has published five collections of poetry with The Gallery Press, Ireland—the most recent of which is *Only This Room* (2009)— as well as two novels, *Hannie Bennett's Winter Marriage* and *The Bird Woman*, both of which have appeared in the UK and the USA. Her web publication can be found at http://chapbooks.webdelsol.com/worldvoices/hardie/swim.html. She has won many prizes, including the Lawrence O'Shaughnessy Award for Irish Poetry; the Michael Hartnett Award; and the Patrick and Katherine Kavanagh Award for Poetry. *Selected Poems* is due in Ireland from the Gallery Press and in the UK from Bloodaxe in 2011. She is a member of Aosdána.

MARIE HEANEY was born in County Tyrone. She trained as a teacher and began her career as a teacher in schools in Northern Ireland. In 1972 she moved with her family to Wicklow and later to Dublin where she now lives. She is the author of *Over Nine Waves: a Book of Irish Legends* which is published by Faber and Faber. She has also written a book of Irish legends for children, *The Names Upon the Harp*, illustrated by PJ Lynch also published by Faber and Faber. In her capacity as an editor at TownHouse Publishing, Dublin, she edited *Sources: Letter from Irish People on Sustenance for the Soul* and *Heart Mysteries*, a short anthology of poems from Ireland. She has also edited three collections from RTÉ's *Sunday Miscellany*. She has contributed to newspapers and journals and has written for radio and television. She is married and has three children.

BIDDY JENKINSON is, at present, engaged in creating a safe haven for bumblebees and in meditations on her relationship with the Muse. An rún atá aici: bheith ag gáirí. An leabhar filíochta is deireanaí dá cuid is ea *Oíche Bhealtaine* (Coiscéim 2005). Late in 2010 Coiscéim publish *Duinnín ar an Sceilg*, a second collection of her detective stories featuring Duinnín, the lexicographer (go maithe sé di é!), and a third book in the series for children (and for those who read for them) featuring Púca as hero. She has won the Buler Award, and many Oireachtas awards.

SEÁN LYSAGHT was born in 1957 and grew up in Limerick. He was educated at UCD, where he studied French and English. He has published six collections of poetry and a biography of the naturalist Robert Lloyd Praeger (1865-1953), *The Life of a Naturalist* (Four Courts Press, 1998). His recent collections include *The Mouth of a River* (2007), a celebration of the landscape of north Mayo, and a volume of translations from Goethe, *Venetian Epigrams* (2008), both from the Gallery Press. In 2007 he received the O'Shaughnessy Award for Poetry. He teaches at GMIT Castlebar and lives in Westport, Co. Mayo.

DEREK MAHON was born in Belfast in 1941, studied at Trinity College, Dublin, and the Sorbonne, and has held journalistic and academic appointments in London and New York. A member of Aosdána, he has received numerous awards including the Irish Academy of Letters Award, the Scott Moncrieff Translation Prize, and Lannan and Guggenheim Fellowships. Publications from The Gallery Press include *The Hudson Letter, The Yellow Book, Words in the Air* (bilingual, with the French of Philippe Jaccottet), *Birds* (a translation of *Oiseaux* by Saint-John Perse), *Harbour Lights* (2005), Winner of the *Irish Times* Poetry Now Award 2006, *Adaptations* (2006), *Life on Earth* (2008) and *An Autumn Wind* (2010). He has also adapted widely for the theatre. His *Collected Poems* appeared in 1999 and a new Penguin *Selected Poems* in 2000. He received the David Cohen Prize 2007, for recognition of a lifetime's achievement in literature.

JOHN MINIHAN was born in Dublin in 1946 and raised in Athy, Co. Kildare and in London. In 1962 he became an apprentice photographer with the *Daily Mail*. He later joined the *Evening Standard*. He returned regularly to Athy in order to record the lives of its inhabitants. More than twenty years of this recording resulted in *Shadows from the Pale* (Secker and Warburg, 1996). His portfolio of literary photographs is extensive. Famous especially for his photographs of Samuel Beckett, whom he met as a result of his Athy photographs, Minihan has exhibited around the world, and is currently working on a project involving Irish-Americans in New York and Boston. He is primarily a film photographer, and uses a Rolleiflex camera.

EILÉAN NÍ CHUILLEANÁIN was born in 1942 in Cork, and educated in Cork and Oxford. She is Associate Professor of English, Trinity College, Dublin, where she has taught since 1966. She has researched and published academic work on the literature of the English Reformation, on Irish literature 1750-1900, and on translation. She was co-founder with Macdara Woods, Leland Bardwell and Pearse Hutchinson of the literary magazine *Cyphers*. Her *Selected Poems* was published by Gallery Press and Faber in 2008; her latest book, *The Sun-fish*, was awarded the Griffin International Prize for poetry in 2010. She has translated poetry from several languages, in particular *The Water Horse* from the Irish of Nuala Ní Dhomhnaill, with Medbh McGuckian, and *After the Raising of Lazarus* from the Romanian of Ileana Mălăncioiu. She is currently working on translations from Irish and Italian. She is married to the poet Macdara Woods, and they have one son, Niall, a musician. They live in Dublin and sometimes in Umbria.

NUALA NÍ DHOMHNAILL was born in 1952 and grew up in the Irish-speaking areas of West Kerry and in Tipperary. She studied at University College, Cork, and now lives in Dublin. She has published four collections of poems in Irish, *An Dealg Droighin* (Cló Mercier, 1981), *Féar Suaithinseach* (An Sagart, 1984), *Feis* (An Sagart, 1991) and *Cead Aighnis* (An Sagart, 1998). The Gallery Press has published four collections of her poems, with translations into English, *Pharoah's Daughter* (Bilingual, translations by thirteen writers, 1990), *The Astrakhan Cloak* (Bilingual, translations by Paul Muldoon, 1992), *The Water Horse* (Bilingual, translations by Medbh McGuckian and Eiléan Ní Chuilleanáin, 1999) and *The Fifty Minute Mermaid* (Bilingual, translations by Paul Muldoon, 2007). She received the 1988 O'Shaughnessy Award for Poetry and the 1991 American Ireland Fund Literary Award. She served as visiting professor of Irish Studies at NYU and Boston College in 1999. She was Ireland Professor of Poetry from 2002 to 2004. She is a member of Aosdána.

BERNARD O'DONOGHUE was born in Cullen, Co. Cork and still lives there for part of the year. He moved to England in 1962; since 1965 he has lived in Oxford where he teaches medieval English at Wadham

College. He has published five books of poems; his *Selected Poems* was published by Faber in 2008. He has also published critical studies of both contemporary and medieval poetry, as well as a verse translation of *Sir Gawain and the Green Knight* (Penguin, 2006). He was the winner of the Whitbread Poetry Prize (1995) and the Cholmondeley Award (2009).

CATHAL Ó SEARCAIGH was born "faoi scáth na hEargaile" in Donegal, where he still lives. Among his recent publications are *Seal i Neipeal* (Cló Iar-Chonnachta, 2004), *Oíche Dhrochghealaí* (Coiscéim, 2005), a play, *Mairimid leis na Mistéirí agus drámaí eile* (Arlen House, 2005), *Gúrú i gClúidíní* (Cló Iar-Chonnachta, 2006) and *Light on Distant Hills: a Memoir* (Simon & Schuster, 2009). He won the Irish Times Literature Award in 2000 and was awarded the Ireland Fund Literary Award in 2007. *By the Hearth in Mín A' Leá* (Arc Publications, 2005) was a Poetry Book Society translation Choice in 2006. He is the Irish Language Editor of *Irish Pages*, and is a member of Aosdána.

MACDARA WOODS was born in Dublin in 1942. He has published 16 books, mainly poetry, as well as collaborating with composers and performers on a number of CDs and also with graphic artists. Most recent collections: *Artichoke Wine* (Dedalus Press, 2006) and a 2007 reprint by Dedalus of *Knowledge in the Blood: New and Selected Poems* originally published in 2000. He has read his work from Berkeley in California to the Gorki Institut, Moscow, and Moscow State University, and in between. Most recently he has read in Brazil, Argentina and Turkey. His work has been translated into more than a dozen languages. His next collection, *The Cotard Syndrome*, is due from Dedalus in 2011. He was a founder-editor of the literary journal *Cyphers*. A member of Aosdána, he lives in Dublin, and when he can, in Umbria. The operation anticipated at the end of his contribution to this book has since been successfully carried out.

Dedalus Press
Poetry from Ireland and the world

Established in 1985, the Dedalus Press is one of Ireland's best-known literary imprints, dedicated to new Irish poetry and to poetry from around the world in English translation.

For further information on Dedalus Press titles, as well as audio samples and podcasts in our Audio Room, please visit **www.dedaluspress.com**.

"One of the most outward looking poetry presses in Ireland and the UK"
—UNESCO.org